SECRET SEX WARS

SECRET SEX WARS

A BATTLE CRY FOR PURITY

GENERAL EDITOR, ROBERT S. SCOTT, SR.

MOODY PUBLISHERS
CHICAGO

© 2008 by
ROBERT S. SCOTT SR., GENERAL EDITOR

Editor: Kathryn Hall
Cover Design: TS Design Studio
Interior Design: Ragont Design

Library of Congress Cataloging-in-Publication Data

Secret sex wars : a battle cry for purity / Robert S. Scott, Sr., general editor.
    p. cm.
Includes bibliographical references (p.   ).
ISBN-13: 978-0-8024-8551-9
ISBN-10: 0-8024-8551-0
   1. Sex—Religious aspects—Christianity. 2. Christian men—Sexual behavior. I. Scott, Robert S., Sr.

BT708.S25 2008
241'.66—dc22

2008000831

1 3 5 7 9 10 8 6 4 2

Printed in the United States of America.

To our sons,

H.B. Charles III
Paul Wesley Felix, Jr.
William Josiah, and Robert S. Scott Jr.
Joshua K.L., and Brian E. Kennedy Jr.
Jonathan Paul, Isaiah Andrew, and Timothy James Kidd
Jordan Anthony, Joseph Anthony,
and Justin Anthony Hargrove
Jonathan Gibran, Josiah Gibran;
Jeremiah Gibran and Joshua Gibran Sholar

our prayer is that you will find satisfaction in God's grace
as you grow and follow the principles in this book
and as you follow our example
as men in pursuit of God in all of His holiness.

CONTENTS

FOREWORD

IN my humble opinion, Muhammed Ali was the greatest boxer to ever live. He completely understood the sport, both the mental as well as physical aspects. The fact that he attacked his opponent from multiple fronts made him formidable. He placed his contenders on the defensive by taunting them verbally outside of the ring, creating doubts and delusions, and then meeting them already mentally defeated in the ring, isolated from their supportive entourage. The Enemy of our souls (Satan) uses a similar strategy on men today. As it relates to sexual purity, many men find themselves defeated. The Enemy has attacked them in isolation through pornography, and is beating them up mentally through shame and guilt and physically through the lie of illicit sexual experiences.

It is imperative that we inform both young and mature men of certain things to avoid. First of all, never enter a spiritual battle alone. Always remember that the Devil seeks to isolate you so that he can freely cut you with his stinging punches.

In order to overcome the onslaught of sexual temptation, there must be a good offense. Along with the Spirit of God, the Word of God, and the body of Christ, this book is a tremendous addition to your arsenal. *Secret Sex Wars: A Battle Cry for Purity* is the combined wisdom of a group of brothers who offer tried biblical solutions to help us when we find ourselves in the ring staring at a fierce opponent.

As we all know, you do not prepare for a fight on the morning of the fight, but you prepare a lifetime for those few minutes in the ring. This book has been created to help you prepare. As an older man who strives to fight the good fight every day, I have many books I consider personal friends. I believe this book can be such a book for you.

As children we fought in secret, behind the school, to avoid the watchful eye of the principal. When it comes to the formidable enemy of sexual temptation, we must not fight alone in private, but always involve the Bible, prayer, and books like this one that have been written by godly men.

My brother, as you battle in your fight for moral purity, realize that with the Lord's help, you can "float like a butterfly and sting like a bee." Use this book as a trusted friend. Make notes in it and highlight useful passages. And always remember that Jesus is the referee in the fight and He has promised that you will never encounter a temptation that is more powerful than you are (1 Corinthians 10:13).

Dr. Harold D. Davis
Executive Director of TALKS Mentoring Ministry
Champaign, IL

INTRODUCTION

— Paul W. Felix,
  President of the Los Angeles
  Bible Training School
— Pastor-Teacher Robert S. Scott Sr.,
  General Editor

YOU might ask, "Why another book on sexual purity?" More than a few have already been written, and some of them are quite good. The short answer is that as long as the blaze of immorality continues to burn out of control, destroying our families, churches, and communities, we must keep trying to put the fire out. The harsh reality is that this devastating inferno has been raging long enough and the time is now for it to cease.

On May 20, 1985, President Ronald Reagan asked Attorney General Edwin Meese III "to form a Commission of Pornography . . . to determine the nature, extent, and impact on society of pornography in the United States . . . and to make specific recommendations . . . concerning more effective ways in which the spread of pornography could be contained."[1] One of the primary concerns of that report was how the use of modern technology could have the potential to exacerbate the problem by making pornography so readily available.

Some twenty or so years later, the report seems prophetic in its unheeded cries to plug the breach before the dam bursts. On February 6, 2006, Reuters released a report that defies comprehension. It claimed that of 2,500 students surveyed in Canada, "87% of university students are having sex over webcams, instant messenger, or the telephone."[2] Technology has infested every corner of our society with a pornographic virus. As of the writing of this book, current statistics show that "the total porn industry revenue for 2006 (was) $13.3 billion in the United States . . . [with] more than 70% of men from 18 to 34 visit[ing] a pornographic site in a typical month."[3] Sadly, this epidemic has also infiltrated the family environment as reported below.

> Two-thirds of the divorce lawyers attending a 2002 meeting of the American Academy of Matrimonial Lawyers said excessive interest in online porn contributed to more than half of the divorces they handled that year. They also said pornography had an almost non-existent role in divorce just seven or eight years earlier. . . . This devastation isn't confined to adults either. The Justice Department estimates that nine of 10 children between the ages of 8 and 16 have been exposed to pornography online.[4]

These are staggering figures. Thirteen billion dollars is more money than the NBA, MLB, and NFL made, combined! It is also more money than NBC, ABC, and CBS made, combined![5] There are about 420 million porn pages on the net. And 40 million Americans regularly visit porn

Web sites.[6] We are living through the *pornification* of our nation; moreover, the collateral damage to our families, churches, and communities is staggering. The frightening truth is, this impending train wreck doesn't appear to be losing any speed. So yes, another book had to be written, as others in the future will be necessary—until we somehow derail this runaway train. The contributing authors of *Secret Sex Wars: A Battle Cry for Purity* felt compelled to address this problem head-on with biblical answers and practical insights that give real hope.

Since these issues affect every man, why write a book on purity specifically directed toward an African American male readership? The answer is, none of the contributing authors of this book feel that the rampant immorality in our nation is what one might call, "a black thing." The problems addressed in this book are universal. They transcend every ethnic, economic, and educational segment of our society. However, precisely because the plague is so pervasive, it most certainly does exist in the urban community that God has called us to serve.

As witnesses to the devastation that immorality is causing in our community,[7] we are compelled to respond. All of the contributors are African American men who have a burden to reach out to our brothers who struggle with these sins. All of us have counseled couples whose marriages were being torn apart by immorality. We have experienced the pain of losing brothers who became POWs (prisoners of war) to sexual sins; that is, brothers who once stood shoulder to shoulder with us in the battles of ministry. We have been wounded by the news that another son of the church has become ensnared by the seductive power of illicit sex.

Our response as fellow brothers is to help carry our fellow fallen brothers' burdens. Therefore, in April of 2005, we hosted a men's conference, sponsored in part by the Los Angeles Bible Training School, called "Living Pure in an Impure World." Approximately three hundred men, predominantly African Americans, gathered on a Friday and Saturday. Throughout this Spirit-filled time, we wrestled with God to bless us. Many brothers opened up about their struggles, found hope in God's Word, and gained victory through Christ's enablement. It became apparent that the time had come for a book specifically addressed to African American brothers who want victory in their personal battles for purity.

Finally, let us address one more related question: why a book entitled *Secret Sex Wars?* We have not written *a tell-all* exposé of who is doing what and who they are doing it with. Although a book of dirty little secrets might sell well, it won't help anybody win their struggle to gain purity. This book is entitled *Secret Sex Wars* because the Word of God is clear that the longer we try to keep our struggles with immorality a secret, the longer they will defeat us. The Bible clearly describes this dilemma.

> *When I kept silent **about my sin**, my body wasted away through my groaning all day long. For day and night Your hand was heavy upon me; my vitality was drained away as with the fever heat of summer. Selah. I acknowledged my sin to You, and my iniquity I did not hide; I said, "I will confess my transgressions to the LORD"; and You forgave the guilt of my sin. Selah. (Psalm 32:3–5)*

Brothers, the time is long overdue for us to bring this secret into the light. Everyone sees the consequences, so we need to stop pretending that we don't know what's going on. In the following pages, you will find straight talk, real hope, and biblical answers that will help you walk in purity as God designed. All of the contributors of this book have wrestled with the question: what does the Bible say? on this subject. We know that God will bless you if you heed the divine instruction presented in this book. It was written to give you one answer—the Word of God. If you've tried everything else (whether you've struggled just a little or whether you feel like you've already lost the battle), we plead with you to try God's Word. It alone has the power to change lives and set sinners free.

Even if you don't consider yourself to be a reader, we plead with you to read this book. Each chapter was written with you in mind, and each one was written to stand alone. Therefore, you don't have to read this book all the way through from front to back. Read it in whatever order you like. Just read, and read prayerfully.

We also want to encourage our sisters to share these books with their sons, brothers, and the other men in your lives. We are more than confident that this book can make a difference because the truths we share here are eternal. We know this firsthand because God has used these battle plans in our lives to enable us to walk in purity. In fact, as the general editor of this project, in part, I believe that God allowed me to participate in this book because through me He clearly illustrates His transforming power to set men free from being enslaved to sexual sin. Brothers, we are praying for you that God will likewise deliver you and give you victory over your sex wars.

SLAYING THE FIERY BEAST

❶ The Foundation for a Successful Battle Plan

John 17:17; 1 Timothy 1:8–10; 1 Timothy 4:6–7

— Pastor Anthony D. Kidd

I T was a typical Lord's Day morning. I woke up excited and looked forward to going to church. I enjoyed being with the Lord's people and worshiping God with them. My hope, though, was that this time would be different. Not that my worship experience wasn't consistently inspiring, but I desired to hear from God, especially since the night before had been so difficult.

You see, that Saturday night I had another episode; an episode that I despised with all of my soul, and one that I was becoming all too familiar with. I was a new believer, having been marvelously converted by God's grace and seeking to live my life in a manner pleasing to Him. Jesus Christ was now my Lord and Savior, and I loved Him for saving me. So much had changed in my life, which could only be explained by the power of God. But not everything had changed; at least not right away. The wanton desires that I had given into and indulged from my late teenage years into early adulthood were still powerfully raging in my heart. And to my surprise I was engaged in an intense battle—a battle that seemed to grow more intense with each passing week.

That battle was with pornography. I knew it was a sin, and I knew God did not want me to view it, but there I was again that night, lurking by the magazine rack at the liquor store across the street from my apartment. With my heart pounding, I tried to convince myself that I was there just to get a soda and some chips, but deep down inside I knew why I was there. I was there because in my heart there was a smoldering fire that beckoned to be set ablaze by the spark of pornographic images. I peeked, I looked, I gazed, I purchased; suddenly, the smoldering embers of lust were set on fire, and well, there I was again.

So I hoped that on this Sunday I might hear something in the sermon that would help me in my struggle. Unfortunately, I had hoped in vain. Don't get me wrong, brothers, I had a good time at church that day—I always did. The music moved me, the sermon inspired me, the praise lifted me, the fellowship encouraged me, and I walked away feeling really good. I felt hopeful. I felt clean again. But it wasn't long before I felt the heat from the embers of lust beginning to smolder in my heart again. And as I tried to resist, it was as if I was trying to put out a raging forest fire with a water pistol. I simply did not possess whatever it took to slay the fiery beast that was now my master, or so I thought.

That was in 1992, and by the grace of God, the fiery beast has since been slain. And with the exception of an occasional spark, the fire has been extinguished. If you're reading this book, you probably know something of the battle of which I speak. Your battle may be with pornography, masturbation, adultery, phone sex, or some other illicit sexual behavior forbidden by Scripture. Whatever the case, by the grace of God, you can experience the same victory that I know and enjoy today. So how did I do it? How can you do it? Brothers, the answer is not as complicated as the Enemy would have you believe. It is also marvelously liberating.

THE CONNECTION

Fed up with what seemed to be a losing battle, I cried out to the Lord in utter desperation. If I was truly a Christian, and Jesus Christ was as powerful as I believed Him to be, then I knew that my frequent moral failures were not His will for me. So I turned to the Scriptures, and there it was. Brothers, it was as if I had never read this particular verse before, even though I had actually read it several times. The words jumped off the page and grabbed me, filling my heart with hope because of what it said and from whose lips it came. They were the words of Jesus, spoken to His Father saying, "Sanctify them in the truth; Your word is truth" (John 17:17). There it was! The connection that I had missed; the connection that nobody had told me about. It was the connection between the *truth* of God's Word and the *sanctification* of God's people—the sanctification that I so desperately desired in the area of sexual purity. So that connection set me on a search in which I discovered new hope and sufficient power to win my battle against lust and pornography.

I pored over my Bible, trying to find other texts that would shed light on Jesus' words in John 17:17. To my joyful surprise, text after text made the same connection—the connection between truth and purity. For instance,

> How can a young man keep his way **pure?** By keeping it **according to Your word.** With all my heart I have sought You; do not let me wander from Your commandments. **Your word** I have treasured in my heart, that **I may not sin against You.** (Psalm 119:9–11)

> If anyone advocates a different doctrine and does not agree with sound words, those of our Lord Jesus Christ, and with **the doctrine conforming to godliness.**
> (1 Timothy 6:3)

> Paul, a bond-servant of God and an apostle of Jesus Christ, for the faith of those chosen of God and the knowledge of **the truth which is according to godliness.**
> (Titus 1:1)

> But we know that the Law is good, if one uses it lawfully, realizing the fact that law is not made for a righteous person, but for those who are lawless and rebellious, for the ungodly and sinners, for the unholy and profane, for those who kill their fathers or mothers, for murderers and **immoral men** and **homosexuals** and kidnappers and liars and perjurers, and whatever else is **contrary to sound**[1] **teaching.** (1 Timothy 1:8–10)

Brothers, what these texts are saying is that "Your [God's] word," "the doctrine," "the truth," and "sound teaching," produces godliness in the lives of God's people. All of these phrases collectively refer to the whole body of pure scriptural instruction. To put it in a more theologically precise way, orthodoxy produces orthopraxy; that is, healthy doctrine promotes healthy living. These texts point out that there is a dynamic connection between doctrine and lifestyle. Take, for example, the 1 Timothy 1:8–10 passage. Having listed a rap sheet of vices that should make even a hardened criminal blush, the apostle Paul argues that those vices and others like them are "contrary to sound teaching."

Paul is not only saying that these vices do not match with what sound teaching says, but more fundamentally, he is saying that these vices are against what sound teaching promotes and produces. Do you see it, brothers? Immorality and homosexuality are "contrary" to healthy doctrine. So if you are a man who persists in these types of vices, among other things, you must ask yourself whether or not you are receiving a regular diet of sound doctrine upon which you are building your life. In all likelihood, according to Paul, the answer is that you are not. For if you were, your lifestyle would not be so contrary to your doctrine.

Now, to be sure, there are men who are familiar with sound doctrine and even teach it, who still engage in illicit sexual sins. Theologians, Bible teachers, professors, and pastors alike, are by no means absent from the sad list of men who have left behind the wreckage of destroyed families, the carnage of ruined reputations, and the scandal of stunned congregations because of immorality. Even the soundest of churches are not immune to these tragedies.

So how can this be? you ask. I submit to you that these men do not know sound doctrine as they should. Experience cannot be the test of truth in these cases. God's Word makes this connection, and we must believe it. Sound doctrine will promote and produce godliness if we know it properly and follow it faithfully. But a man can be exposed to sound doctrine and even agree with it but still not benefit from it just as a chef can cook and serve healthy food to others without personally benefiting from it. He must eat it for himself.

And you, my brother, must eat sound doctrine for yourself. In fact, later in Paul's letter to Timothy, he tells him that the very means by which Timothy will set himself apart as "a good servant of Christ Jesus" will be to constantly *nourish* himself on "sound doctrine" (see 1 Timothy 4:6). So just as healthy food nourishes and promotes a healthy body, in the same way, healthy doctrine nourishes and promotes a healthy soul—a soul not weak and easily susceptible to the infections and diseases of sexual immorality and impurity.

Brother, your soul needs nourishment in order for you to fight your battles against lust and sexual temptation. Victory will not come easily. It takes strength, energy, and focused discipline. That's why in the next verse Paul tells Timothy to "have nothing to do with worldly fables fit only for old women. [But] on the other hand, *discipline*[2] yourself for the purpose of godliness . . ." (1 Timothy 4:7). You must not miss this. In verse 6, Paul mentions the nourishment of the "words of the faith and of the sound doctrine," and in verse 7, he tells Timothy to discipline himself "for the purpose of godliness."

It is the nourishment from the words of the faith and from sound doctrine that will give Timothy the energy and strength he needs to engage in the strenuous discipline of pursuing godliness. Possessing godliness and sexual purity takes discipline, and discipline takes effort, and effort takes energy. Moreover, sound doctrine is an essential component of the fuel that God has ordained to give you that energy. But sadly, brothers, many of us spend our time dabbling "with worldly fables fit only for old women" as Paul warned Timothy in verse 7. It's no small wonder that sexual immorality is rampant among men in our churches.

Therefore, brothers, let me stress again, sound doctrine does not automatically produce purity. Passively sitting under sound doctrine will no more produce sexual purity in your life than passively sitting in a gym will put muscles on your body. There is a biblical process known as progressive sanctification.[3] In this process, the believer daily works out the grace of God in his life as he responds to God's enabling power through trust and obedience. Each man has the responsibility to exercise faith in sound doctrine so that he might experience its sanctifying effect.[4] But the effect is impossible to achieve if, in fact, one's doctrine is not sound.

Even the psalmist of old recognized this dynamic connection. Notice how precisely the psalmist speaks with regard to desiring purity. He asks, "How can a young man keep his way *pure?*" (Psalm 119:9a). This is the million dollar question, is it not? In a moment of utter desperation you've probably asked the same question, haven't you? Look at his answer and let the Spirit of God burn it into your soul. He writes, "By keeping it according to Your word" (Psalm 119:9b). The psalmist knew that if he were to have any success in living a life of purity he would have to live in line with and in dependence upon God's Word. He was so convinced of that reality that he literally "treasured" God's Word in his heart so that he would not become a prisoner in the war against sin (see Psalm 119:11).

Here then, was a man, brothers, who knew the connection between God's Word and a life of purity. Do you share that same connection? Are you experiencing the fruit of that connection? Or are you experiencing the fruit of being under unhealthy doctrine—doctrine which is giving you neither foundation nor power to win your battle against sexual impurity? My brother, it doesn't have to be that way!

THE MISTAKE

Looking back on those early days of my Christian walk, I realize now that I made a fatal mistake—a mistake that cost me dearly. By not recognizing the essential place that sound doctrine plays in a life of purity, I tried to fight the enemy outside of me without first being equipped to capture and hold at bay the enemy within. I involved myself in what Paul refers to as "self-made religion and self-abasement and severe treatment of the body, [which are] of no value against fleshly indulgence" (Colossians 2:23).

I thought it was all up to me to fight in my own strength. So, like many brothers, I majored on what I could do instead of focusing on understanding what Jesus Christ had already done for me. In my futile self-effort to abstain from sexual sin, I was like a man continually walking around the edge of an open pit trying not to fall in. Eventually, I'd get so dizzy from going around in circles, I'd fall right in. To make matters worse, Sunday after Sunday, all I was hearing was, "don't," "stop," "quit," but I wasn't hearing anything about the motivation for, or the power behind "how?" Consequently, the "just say no" approach didn't work for me, as I suspect it isn't working for you either.

Over time, I came to realize that without the sound doctrine necessary to renew my mind, cleanse my heart, inform my conscience, and empower my will, I was simply fighting a spiritual battle using fleshly weapons which proved to be of no effect. I was trying to build a fortress to stand against the attacks of sexual lust not realizing that Jesus Christ and His Word are the only solid foundation upon which my fortress could stand (see Matthew 7:24–25). And without the understanding of His Word as my foundation, my pitiful fortress was as sturdy as a straw house built on the sand—

constantly threatened and easily blown over by the huffing and puffing and blowing of temptation and fleshly desires.

Remember, brothers, any strategy that you adopt to wage the war against impurity must be grounded in, flow from, and be in accordance with sound doctrine. If it is not, you will simply find yourself fighting a losing battle, or even worse, being self-deceived into thinking that temporary moral reform is the same as genuine grace that brings about growth in purity.

FIRST THINGS FIRST

So where does one begin? The answer is, with the Gospel. My brothers, if you are going to experience and maintain any level of victory over lust and impurity, you must first know and believe the true Gospel. It all starts here, for it is the good news of the Gospel that brings you into a vital relationship with God through Jesus Christ. It is the Gospel that defines what that relationship is to be. And it is the Gospel that sustains and builds that relationship. It is the only relationship by which you will be able to stand victorious over the soul-destroying effects of Internet porn, masturbation, being on the down-low, and other sexual sins.

The Bible contains the Gospel, the story of God's good news to humanity. That story is centered in the person of His Son, Jesus Christ, and focused on what He did two thousand years ago on a bloody cross. God is the sovereign and holy Creator of all things, and He created humans in His own image with the privileged capacity to have fellowship with Him in love and obedience. But the first humans ruined that relationship by sinning against God and incurring His just condemnation. Their punishment was separation from God as they took on the nature of sin.

This judgment by God put mankind into the inescapable prison of sin and despair. The Bible teaches that men, even at their best, can only muster up filthy rags before God. Without salvation through Christ, men are enslaved to sin, servants of Satan, and enemies of God. We all deserve temporal and eternal damnation for our rebellious nature and behavior, and apart from the gracious saving activity of God in Christ, that's exactly what each one of us would have received.[5]

The good news is that God graciously took the initiative to provide a way for sinners to be forgiven and restored to fellowship with Him. God entered this world in the person of Jesus Christ, the eternal Son of God, to do for sinners what they are impotent to do for themselves. Having lived the perfect life, Jesus died a sacrificial death on the cross as a substitute for lawbreaking rebels. It was on that cross that Jesus paid in full the price for sins so that sinners might be forgiven by God. He satisfied the just claims of the law of God so that sinners might be justified by God and absorbed the awful wrath of God so that sinners might be reconciled to God. Then, having triumphed over sin, on the third day Jesus rose from the dead, gaining victory over death and the grave. And now, as the resurrected Lord and King, He is graciously offering salvation to all who will repent of their sins and believe solely on Him for a right relationship with God.[6] Brothers, this is good news, and it all starts here.

Is this the Gospel that you believe? Is this the good news that is preached and taught at your church? Is this the storyline that is being reinforced and emphasized from the pulpit that you sit under? When you stand before God, will it be this Gospel that you cast your hope upon or will it be some other gospel? Listen to me, brothers. You can fight as hard as humanly possible against lust and sexual temptation, but it will be all for naught if you miss it here. And that, my brothers, would be the worst of all casualties of war. Take a moment now and make sure you are trusting in the Lord Jesus Christ as He is presented and offered to you in the Gospel of the Holy Bible.

PRACTICE WHAT YOU BELIEVE

History teaches us that no war can ever be won by accident. Any general taking his soldiers off to battle will have a thoroughly constructed battle plan. Furthermore, he will make sure that each of his men know and execute that plan so that victory can be achieved. Well, it is not much different in our war against sexual impurity. Jesus Christ is our commander-in-chief, and He has given to all His soldiers the perfect war plan. It's called the Bible, and contained in it are doctrines that are foundational for His men to know and believe in order to achieve victory. But just like any successful war plan, it must be followed to the letter. If not, battles are lost, ground is given up, morale is low, and casualties are sustained.

This means that ignorance is not bliss, nor is it acceptable; on the contrary, it is deadly. Therefore, it should be no surprise to us that ignorance is one of Satan's most effective strategies to keep us in bondage to sexual sin. If you don't know God's plan for purity, you can't practice it. This makes it essential for you to give yourself to the study of the Scriptures in order to know how to fight. Look closely at this all-important text:

Seeing that His [God's] divine power has granted to us everything pertaining to life and godliness, through the true knowledge of Him who called us by His own glory

followed to the letter... everything

and excellence. For by these He has granted to us His precious and magnificent promises, so that by them you may become partakers of the divine nature, having escaped the corruption that is in the world by lust. (2 Peter 1:3–4)

Do you see it here, brothers? The apostle Peter has the answer to how we can escape from the prison of corruption that is found in worldly lusts. His answer is, "through the true knowledge of Him [God]" by which we get "His precious and magnificent promises" (vv. 3–4). And it is "by them" that we then grow in Christlikeness. As a result, the more like Christ we become, the less we will lose the battles against sexual temptation and defiling lusts. So then, the key is to embrace the promises that lead us into a deeper knowledge of God because to really know God is to become more like God. But if we do not know the promises of God, which are in His Word, how can we grow in Christlikeness? That's the problem. We can't. We must know God's promises and stand on them in order to partake of them.

Now, you might be thinking that it takes much more than simply knowing some doctrines and promises of Scripture to win the war against sexual sins. In one sense you would be correct, but in another you would be wrong. There is more to the strategy of Christ's war plan. He has given to us a multiarrayed arsenal to ensure our victory, and you will become more acquainted with those weapons as you read the other chapters of this book. But do not underestimate the power of knowing sound doctrine and the Word of God. Let me give you two examples of what I mean, one from the apostle Paul and another from the apostle John.

In Paul's first letter to the Corinthian church, he deals with a myriad of issues. As you read the letter, it's as if he is writing to the contemporary church in America. The church is worldly, immature, doctrinally unstable, and awash with sensuality and sexual sin of the grossest sort. In the second part of chapter 6, Paul deals with a group of men in the church who were apparently visiting prostitutes at the local pagan temple. He writes,

> Do you not **know** that your bodies are members of Christ? Shall I then take away the members of Christ and make them members of a prostitute? May it never be! Or do you not **know** that the one who joins himself to a prostitute is one body with her? For He says, "THE TWO SHALL BECOME ONE FLESH" [emphasis original]. But the one who joins himself to the Lord is one spirit with Him. Flee immorality. Every other sin that a man commits is outside the body, but the immoral man sins against his own body. Or do you not **know** that your body is a temple of the Holy Spirit who is in you, whom you have from God, and that you are not your own? For you have been bought with a price: therefore glorify God in your body. (1 Corinthians 6:15–20)

Brothers, this is as scandalous as it gets. Immorality, prostitution, adultery—it's all here. So how does Paul deal with it? He appeals to what they should have known. He gives them a command, and in doing so, he gives them the doctrines concerning Christ upon which the command can be carried out. Notice that three different times Paul asks the Corinthians if they "know" something. He's assuming that they should have known, but since they didn't, they were committing gross immorality. Their ignorance was leading to their sin. And, brothers, I submit to you, that if you are continually engaging in sexual sins, it is, at least in part, because you do not know something that you should.

Or, perhaps you are not informed in the way that you should be; namely, through sound doctrine.

So Paul reminds the Corinthians of the truth of who they are in Christ Jesus. They are members of Christ (v. 15), one with Christ (v. 17), and purchased by Christ (vv. 19–20). In essence, he reminds them of the doctrines of *the spiritual union with Christ* and *redemption*. Paul's point is that each of these doctrines has sanctifying implications for the Corinthians in serving to liberate them from the enslaving power of immorality. So when he commands them to "flee immorality" (v. 18), it is a command that rests on the foundation of the sound doctrine that he has explained to them and reminded them of.

They can flee immorality because God has already set them free by purchasing them out of the slave market of sin and joined them to Jesus Christ. And the same is true for you, my brother. You too can flee immorality. But, if you do not know and understand the doctrines behind why and how you can achieve this most important goal, you will continue to struggle with sexual sin. This is why it is so important for you to be in a place where the whole truth of God's pure Word is preached and taught. Consider this, when was the last time you heard a sermon on the believer's union with Christ? Or when was the last time in Bible study you actually were taught the spiritual implications of being redeemed by Christ? It is my hope that you are regularly being taught these and other biblical doctrines so that you can know and experience the victory that is yours in Christ.

Now, let's turn our attention to the first epistle of John. In the first few verses of 1 John 3, the apostle encourages his readers to meditate on the profound reality of the love of God. In doing so, he calls their attention to the second coming of Jesus Christ: "We know that when He appears, we will be like Him, because we will see Him just as He is" (v. 2b). What's important to see here is how John teaches that there is a connection between the doctrine of the second coming and the purity of God's people. Notice in the next verse he writes, "And everyone who has this hope fixed on Him *purifies* himself, just as He is pure" (1 John 3:3).

This is so clear. Knowing, believing, and being focused on the doctrine of the second coming of Jesus Christ is to be motivated and empowered to live a life of purity. Why? Because according to John, only he who practices righteousness will have confidence before the Lord at His coming having given evidence that he is truly born of God; and conversely, he who practices unrighteousness will shrink away from the Lord in shame (see 1 John 2:28–29). The reality of the doctrine promotes and produces the purity!

As with these texts, we see over and again this all-important connection between what we believe and how we behave. Consequently, I am persuaded that in this battle for sexual purity there is arguably no greater way to spend your time and effort than in studying your Bible and committing yourself to learning sound doctrine. Do not fall prey to the prevailing thought that has insidiously made its way into so many of our churches that says, "Doctrine divides; don't focus on it." Yes, it divides all right. It divides the brothers who are serious about glorifying God and honoring Christ with lives of moral purity from the ones who have waved the white flag of surrender to the Enemy of God's people. To the latter, the battle cry is to burn that white flag and pick up the bloodstained banner of Christ, for we are more than conquerors in the Lord Jesus. Brothers, we are on the winning side!

WATCH OUT FOR LAND MINES

Satan is a formidable enemy. He will use whatever means necessary to destroy your life so that you might bring shame on the name of the Lord Jesus. In addition to trying to keep you ignorant of sound doctrine, he also corrupts doctrine through false teaching. He knows that if you will unknowingly embrace his doctrines, which Paul calls "doctrines of demons" in 1 Timothy 4:1, you will not only be ineffective in your battle against sexual temptation, but you will also be more susceptible to carnal lusts. The apostle Peter understood this and warned the first-century church with these words,

> But false prophets also arose among the people, just as there will also be false teachers among you, who will secretly introduce destructive heresies, even denying the Master who bought them, bringing swift destruction upon themselves. Many will follow their **sensuality**, and because of them the way of the truth will be maligned. (2 Peter 2:1–2)

Understand this well: bad doctrine not only distorts the way of the truth, but it also corrupts the souls of its hearers by leading its followers to sensuality. Peter further describes it this way, "For speaking out arrogant words of vanity they [false teachers] entice by *fleshly desires*, by *sensuality*, those who barely escape from the ones who live in error" (2 Peter 2:18). False teaching is ruinous to your pursuit of sexual purity, for underpinning it is an inherent carnality which wages war against your soul's genuine longing for moral holiness.

Every time you give yourself to bad doctrine, you are not only undercutting your own ability to live a righteous life, but you are also opening yourself up to being carried away by sinful lust. This is why it is so important to guard yourself from the many subtleties of Satan's deceptions that mask themselves as true teachings of Scripture. The only way you will be successful at doing so is to equip yourself through studying the Word of God so that you will be sensitive to it and alert when you hear doctrine that does not ring of God's truth.

Across the contemporary landscape of American Christianity there are several forms of false doctrine that you need to be aware of if you're going to be successful in your fight against sexual sins. For example, there is a doctrine which claims that Jesus Christ died so that you might indulge your every desire for wealth and material blessings. This false doctrine does nothing but breed carnal lust and greed within your soul. It will be impossible for you to deny yourself when all you're hearing from the preachers who teach this falsehood is to indulge yourself. It does nothing but feed the flesh, the very thing that Jesus called us to put to death.

Make no mistake about it, greed is inextricably connected to immorality and impurity. In one list Paul placed them together along with other sexual sins because he understood this connection: "But immorality or any impurity or *greed* must not even be named among you, as is proper among saints" (Ephesians 5:3). It's clear as a bell. Unmortified greed will bleed out in every area of a man's life, especially in the sexual arena. It is naïve to think that greed can be compartmentalized.

Moreover, if you're sitting under the so-called "prosperity gospel," you are only stoking the embers of the very fire that you desire to put out. Week after week your flesh is being stimulated to crave more and more. Is it any wonder that you're finding it so difficult to keep your passions in check? If you sow to your flesh from the flesh, you will reap corruption, as Galatians 6:8 points out.

Equally harmful to your sexual purity, but far more subtle than the "prosperity gospel" is what I call "radical emotionalism." The danger here is the elevation of emotions to the place of master. It is not that emotions are wrong; they are not. In fact, the Bible places a high premium on them. You cannot serve and worship God properly without them. However, God designed our emotions to be governed by His truth—by sound doctrine. But, in far too many of our churches, the great achievement of many preachers is to get the people as emotionally charged as possible. In many of these settings, sound doctrine is a nonissue, for the people no longer endure sound doctrine but have simply heaped to themselves teachers who tickle their ears and excite their fancies (see 2 Timothy 4:3–4). In this toxic environment, emotions become sovereign and truth is set aside.

Brothers, once you begin to be led by your emotions in this way you will have a difficult time standing on the truth when sexual temptation beckons to your feelings. The man governed by his feelings and not by the truth of God's Word is no match for the fierce power of sexual temptation, no matter how strong he may be. Remember, it was bondage to his own sensual feelings that made the strong man Samson weak when it came to women.[7]

Watch out for these land mines and others as well. Far too many of our fellow comrades have already been blown up by them. Do whatever it takes to put yourself in a healthy context in which the Scriptures are accurately and faithfully taught. Study and learn sound theology, listen to faithful preaching, and read solid Christian books. Together they will assist you in discerning bad doctrine that cripples the soul's ability to fight the good fight of faith.

CONCLUSION

Brothers, I've given you much to absorb. But it's all necessary and foundational. Without being committed to sound doctrine your desire for sexual purity will not be easily fulfilled, if at all. The Lord Jesus Christ has not left us insufficiently equipped to fight and win this war. You do not have to be a prisoner of war in the battle for sexual purity. He has given to us a complete battle plan by which, if faithfully followed, we will know and experience victory. If we do our part, God will do His. Not because He is obligated to respond to us, but because He is gracious and kind, and because He desires our purity more than we even know.

I began this chapter by sharing with you the great connection I found years ago in John 17:17, where Jesus prays that all of His people be sanctified by the truth of God's Word. Let me end by sharing with you a marvelous promise that Jesus makes. It will encourage you to trust His Word in your battle for purity: "If you continue in My word, then you are truly disciples of Mine; and you will know the truth, and the truth will make you free" (John 8:31–32).

→POINTS OF REFLECTION

1. Jesus prayed in John 17:17 for God to sanctify His people by the truth. Do you think God answers that prayer? Of course He does! So, brother, there should be no doubt that the power of God is available to you to experience victory over sexual sins. We learned though that you have a part to play in experiencing that sanctification; namely, learning, believing, and standing on sound doctrine. Read Psalm 119:9–11 and John 8:31–32 carefully, and write out in your own words how important God's Word is to your pursuit of sexual purity.

2. In I Timothy 4:6, Paul mentions being nourished on the words of faith and of sound doctrine. The image is that of receiving nutrition from something you've eaten. It should be clear to you that "sound doctrine" is nutritious and "bad doctrine" is harmful. How are you nourishing yourself on sound doctrine? What steps do you need to take to receive a regular diet of healthy Bible teaching? If you need help getting started, ask your pastor to recommend to you a solid evangelical study Bible such as *The MacArthur Study Bible* and a good evangelical book on Bible doctrine like Bruce Milne's *Know the Truth* or Wayne Grudem's *Systematic Theology*.

3. In your battle for sexual purity, your understanding of the Gospel is critical. It is the Gospel that not only saves you; it is the Gospel that sanctifies you as well. Many brothers fall into the same trap as the Galatian church members by starting off in the Spirit, only to then try to perfect themselves by the flesh (see Galatians 3:1–3). You must learn

how to apply the Gospel to your battle with sexual sins. Carefully read 1 Corinthians 6:9–20 and prayerfully study how Paul applies the Gospel to the Corinthians' situation. Write out how the same truths about what Jesus Christ accomplished on your behalf can be applied to your own situation.

4. The Bible is filled with doctrine, and you might be overwhelmed when thinking about what to study. Let me suggest that in all of your studying that you focus your attention on one area in particular. That area is the grace of God. Simply put, remember that grace is the main ingredient in everything that the Bible teaches about what God in Christ has done for your salvation and promises to do through Christ for your sanctification and glorification. Major on those doctrines.

To get started, read Titus 2:11–14 and reflect on the power of God's grace. The next time you're tempted by sexual sin, remembering this passage and putting your faith in it can help you overcome your temptation. Rest assured, if you sincerely desire to do this, the Holy Spirit will be there to help you remember God's Word and your faith in it will release the power to get the victory.

5. Remember that "where sin increased, grace abounded all the more" (Romans 5:20). Whatever your failures have been, God's grace is available to you through your faith in Christ. There is forgiveness, cleansing, restoration, and power at the throne of grace (see Hebrews 4:14–16). Do not let Satan convince you that your sins are so bad that God won't forgive you or that you're so far gone that God can't help you. The Devil is a liar (John 8:44). Read John 8:1–11;

Hebrews 10:14–18; Ephesians 1:7; Hebrews 7:24–25; Philippians 1:6; and 1 Thessalonians 5:23–24. Meditate on these rich Scriptures that have the power to produce much fruit in your life. Then go and fight the good fight, brother.

FEARING GOD WHEN NO ONE ELSE WOULD KNOW

⬆ A Battle Plan for Secret Temptations
Genesis 39

— Pastor Carl A. Hargrove

TAKE a deep breath and prepare yourself for an avenue of biblical truth taken from the rich life of Joseph, the son of Jacob and a man of integrity. His shining example counters the moral poverty of the world in which we live. It is not very difficult to see that our world is one of drama and sensationalism. It is a world filled with scandal where the culture of the day has spun out of control.

In fact, we live in a *sensuality-saturated; PG=PG17; PG13= R+; R=X-; hip-hop; bling-bling; midriff-bearing; who needs God?; some say, God is not great; no one can tell me to wait— I'm in love; give me my space, Life & Leisure; is the Bible really true?; didn't we come from apes?; religious tolerance for every religion—except Christ's; Enron greed; retire early and do my thing; put on my iPod and iTune you out; Jesus is my buddy;*

that's your thing, I can't judge you; this is my thing, you can't judge me; she's so fine, he's so fine; I like both ways—world.

Now, catch your breath and think about it. This is the world as we know it today, isn't it? It is full of energy but devoid of any spiritual direction. From the corruption of Enron to gangsta rap, our communities have developed a jaded view of God and have little sense of right and wrong anymore. All the personalities and images just mentioned, in some sense, capture the moral bankruptcy of the world and the ensuing temptations that accompany it.

The result is an onslaught of opportunities for spiritual failure to occur in the realm of sexuality. It's as if you are in an arena surrounded by shouts of temptation at every level in the stadium. But despite the calls of temptation, there is hope. Therefore, I will share with you a number of biblical truths that will help you to develop a biblical mind-set that, once developed, will propel you to a life of greater purity. I do hope that is what you desire—greater purity. Of course it is. You are not going to say that you want mediocrity, indifference, or continual failure, right? I trust that you don't.

In this time of glitz and glamour, there are many temptations available—on the Internet, at the movies, on the television, at school, in the home, on billboards, in magazines, on the telephone line, and on your date with someone special or someone you hope might become special. Unless you have isolated yourself from society, you must agree that temptations are everywhere. You would agree that the most powerful ones are those that come in secret places. It is here that you must win the battle because what you do in the secret places is a reflection of your true value system.

My favorite Puritan theologian, John Owen, provides an insight that has been used in many pulpits over the years.

He said, "What a man is in secret, in these private duties, that he is in the eyes of God, and no more."[1]

This is so true. What you are when no one else is there, and no one else would know, is who you really are. Before you read another paragraph, my friend, meditate on this truism, and ask yourself to define the real you. Answer the question: who are you?

ARE THE LIGHTS ON?

The way you are when surrounded by others may not be who you are under the cover of darkness. Isn't it telling that the Scriptures associate deceit, scheming, and sin with the state of darkness? Does the world construct a well-lighted strip bar? Do clubs entertain under bright lights? Do criminals prefer to operate at daybreak? Is insider trading done with full disclosure? Why? People want the cover of night and secrecy under which to live their private lives because they desire to avoid the light of detection.

But the truth is, even if every light in your home is on as you view pornography, you are walking in spiritual darkness. For anyone who claims faith in the Lord Jesus Christ, God has called you to live in the light as He is in the light. To live in Christ is to avoid the darkness of secrecy. While reading this chapter that gleans from the biblical character Joseph and his victory over temptation in Genesis 39, I hope that you will rise to the greater light of righteousness and holiness. I am persuaded that you want more of the light, because you would not otherwise be reading this book; that is, unless you simply enjoy receiving information. That isn't you, correct? No, you are reading it because you want to be a warrior of light and help others walk in that same light. You are called from darkness to light. The Scripture is clear that you are called to walk in the light. Jesus described His desire for us when He said,

> To open their eyes so that they may turn from darkness to light and from the dominion of Satan to God, that they may receive forgiveness of sins and an inheritance among those who have been sanctified by faith in Me. (Acts 26:18)

The apostles further reiterated Jesus' expectation and promises on several occasions:

> For you were formerly darkness, but now you are Light in the Lord; walk as children of Light (for the fruit of the Light consists in all goodness and righteousness and truth). (Ephesians 5:8–9)

> So that you will prove yourselves to be blameless and innocent, children of God above reproach in the midst of a crooked and perverse generation, among whom you appear as lights in the world. (Philippians 2:15)

> But if we walk in the Light as He Himself is in the Light, we have fellowship with one another, and the blood of Jesus His Son cleanses us from all sin. (1 John 1:7)

Friend, let me impress upon you the call of these verses as you move into the body of this chapter. Instead of a flickering light in the midst of darkness, you must be a radiant witness in a world without a spiritual compass. Grasp your call and accept the responsibility to be a *luminary*; that is, a reflection of the light of Jesus Christ in communities gone astray. You must absorb the principles from this book, "man up," and answer the call to die to self (Galatians 2:20).

Many people depend on your light to offer them guidance and to show them the way (Matthew 5:14–16). Your family, neighbors, friends, coworkers, and enemies need you to be a luminary, not a falling star. You should already know that there are consequences to your action or inaction. Never for a moment think that you live without a profound influence on others. When you win your secret battle, you win not only for yourself, but for those you affect now and in the future.

THE BIBLE AND DARK PLACES

We are all faced with temptation. This is the daily course of living in this natural world. Whatever the moral issue we face, every man is susceptible to the temptations of the flesh. Moreover, in our urban centers, the opportunities to meet with the temptations of the world are inflated. It appears that around every corner, there is something lurking, calling, and tempting us to compromise our Christian character. Turn-of-the-century poet and playwright Oscar Wilde once said, "I can handle everything but temptation; the way I deal with it is to yield to it."

Most would say that this is a foolish statement. However, there may have been moments when you have felt the same way concerning a particular struggle. You may have thought that it would be easier to give in rather than to resist. The pressure mounts, emotions rise, testosterone increases, the Spirit is ignored, and another fall occurs![2] Have there been moments when you wanted to resist, you knew it was best to resist, but invariably, you yielded? Everyone has yielded to temptation at some point in their life and wished they had resisted. You look back and say, "what happened? Why didn't I resist? Why couldn't I just say no?"

The Scriptures offer you advice on how to say no to temptation. In the life of Joseph, you see a man who said no even when no one else would have known. The opportunity was ripe to sin. He resisted when temptation sought to stain his character. It is my hope that as you read this chapter you will learn from his life and allow the Word of God to teach you how to handle temptation—especially in those moments when no one else will know if you yield to the cry of temptation. The adage remains true that character is who you are in secret.

THE NATURE OF THE SECRET BATTLE

One of the first ways to ensure that you win the battle against temptation is to develop an understanding of the enemy you are facing. General George Patton was a great commander who successfully engaged the enemy, partly because of his habit of reading the tactics of his foes. He was not naïve to the ways of those who fought against him.

Similarly, the apostle Peter warned his readers that they should know that Satan is like a roaring lion seeking someone to devour (see 1 Peter 5:8). Too many brothers are naïve to Satan's battle plan and are falling prey to his tactics. I am not suggesting that you spend an inordinate amount of time studying the Devil's ways. I have observed this tactic to be a dangerous trend in the church. At times, the people of God spend more time considering the schemes of the Evil One than they do meditating on the Word of God, which will make them strong for the battle (Psalm 19:7–14; 119:25, 50, 93, 107, 154; 2 Timothy 3:15; 1 Peter 2:2–5).

Before I continue, I should also mention this: if you are looking for instruction on how to "bind the devil," learn a "covenant confession," or "crush Satan's neck," then I cannot help you. However, I do propose an investigation into a powerful example from Scripture, from which you can extract biblical principles that will help you resist the next time some allurement seeks to undermine your commitment to Christ. We must avoid shallow, gimmicky confessions and seek the sound application of biblical solutions for the very real struggles that men face.

TEMPTATION'S ENTICEMENTS

My brother, as you battle for purity, the first lesson for developing a proper battle plan is to understand that sin is enticing. In Genesis 39:7, Potiphar's wife enticed Joseph with a golden opportunity according to the world's standard. She had no problem expressing herself. Her sexual revolution started long before the present trend of a woman's sexual freedom.[3] She said to Joseph, "Lie with me." Joseph was a slave and she was the wife of an Egyptian official. It is reasonable to conclude that she was beautiful since she would have been a trophy wife who represented Potiphar's station in life. Consider this thought: a beautiful woman makes a sexual offer when no one else is around. What does a brother do?

Before I give you the options, let's decide what you need to understand in anticipation of a proper response. I could tell you some possible approaches would be to run, hide, stop, etc. However, I want to establish a biblical foundation. Equipped with a biblical answer to enticements, you won't find yourself running, hiding, and stopping, again and again. Sin will entice you to fulfill desires in a manner that dishonors the Gospel that you claim to love. But you can overcome your fleshly desires when you are armed with the truth of God's Word.

Potiphar's wife sought to charm Joseph with her beauty and compliments. The male psyche is drawn to anything that affirms his manhood. The advances of a woman may be the most unrefined form of this type of affirmation. There is something in the flesh that says, "I still have it." Well, unless you develop a different mind-set, you may lose all that you have that is worth keeping.

If a proper reaction is to take place, you must understand that not only is sin enticing, it can be unexpected. In your moment of enticement, the offer of sex is a spiritual obstacle that seeks to redirect you from a course of godliness and truth.

TEMPTATION'S BLINDSIDE

Potiphar's wife attempted to blindside this man of God. Blindsides are the worst hits to take. I know this all too well from my days of high school and college football. Unless you have really good footing and a keen awareness of your opponent, you are going to get knocked off your feet. Look around and count all the men who were running the race but got blindsided. How many apologies from spiritual leaders have you heard in the past decade? But unlike many who have fallen to seduction, Joseph said to her, "You are his wife" (v. 9). In the battle for purity, because the source of your temptation may be unexpected, you must make sure that your spiritual footing is stable (see Ephesians 6:11, 13–14; note the call to "stand firm").

TEMPTATION'S PERSISTENCY

It just won't stop, will it? This characteristic is one that you probably know all too well—temptation is persistent. I say this because unless you have isolated yourself from the real world, you are well aware that temptation is lurking around every corner, and it does not give up. Notice what the Scripture says about Joseph's temptress: "She spoke to Joseph day after day" (v. 10). Temptations come at you like the air raids of the Gulf War with one goal in mind—to collapse your spiritual defenses. My father was a military man (WWII and Korea), and I had aspirations of following in his steps. Several times he told me about how they made a "push" against the enemy. This was a period of heavy bombardment, carried out with hopes of weakening the enemy's forces. Temptation is constantly making a "push" against you and wanting you to collapse under the pressure.

I know that you have been there before, my friend. There is the look you shouldn't have taken, the touch you shouldn't have given, the pop-up screen you should have closed, the kiss you should have waited on that led to the sex that wasn't meant to be, and even the fantasy that replays in your mind. Sin is not going to wait for you to call for help. It will continue its onslaught until you say yes or take the steps necessary to resist.

TEMPTATION'S VULNERABLE MOMENTS

There is another characteristic of temptation that requires spiritual shrewdness if you hope to win the battle for purity. Understand that temptation will often come in your vulnerable moments. Notice the next phrase in the episode: "None of the men of the household was there inside" (v. 11). These are moments when you are unusually exposed—the isolation of your business trip . . . when your parents are away . . . when you are surfing the Internet and no one can see—moments when accountability is extremely low.

There are a hundred different situations that create vulnerability. I am convinced that you know your vulnerable moments. If not, simply recall the contexts in which you compromised your faith. Far too often I have counseled men struggling with sexual sins who know their vulnerable moments but have not taken the required precautions to move from vulnerability to safety. Sometimes these moments come when you are weak emotionally. This is an example I have seen on many occasions: a relationship comes to an end and one or both partners make an emotional rebound with the wrong person, in the wrong way. Subsequently, they make choices that never would have been made when they were stronger emotionally.

My brother, surely you have faced an emotionally vulnerable moment caused by the loss of a job, family challenges, marital concerns, loneliness, or simply the everyday struggles in life that have beaten you down. Then temptation comes along and you yield when you normally wouldn't have. The key is to recognize your vulnerable moments and create safety barriers so that you do not succumb to your areas of weakness.

A WORD OF CAUTION TO THE TRUE WARRIOR

Before we move to the next consideration, I want to highlight a specific vulnerable moment that the true warrior might face. Being aware of this potentially vulnerable situation will help the true warrior to avoid falling.

Some men fall because their character simply catches up to them. Others, who are authentic warriors, sometimes fall because they did not take proper precautions or recognize potential dangers. I am referring to the vulnerability of emotional attachments that begin within a genuine ministry context.

Several situations may lead to vulnerability. Perhaps it can occur when you are counseling a couple, maybe a friend has confided in you, or you are simply engaged in a sincere conversation in which emotional concerns are expressed. In each of these situations, there is the potential for a woman to become emotionally attached to you. In these moments, you represent what she desires and even believes she deserves in a man. You must be discerning enough to know when a woman is emotionally attaching herself to you. I admit that this is subjective, but the results, if unchecked, can be absolutely devastating. This is one reason why I believe a man should not counsel a woman one-on-one. Do not be naïve in this matter. Take precautions and protect your friend's/congregant's emotional integrity. There are wolves in the church who prey on some women's emotional instability. I personally know of ministers in the Los Angeles area who have gained a reputation for doing just that—using their roles as shepherds to take advantage of such vulnerable moments.

What happens in these situations? The counselor/friend becomes the hero the woman longs for. She may create a picture in her mind of a better life with him, and if unguarded, what began as a mere illusion can lead to a fall—one that neither person had intended. The sobering outcome: another fallen warrior is added to the list of losses. Let me challenge you to take the high road. This means that even if you never reciprocate the vibes you sense, be a man of honor and protect that sister's heart by removing yourself from any situation that would create such vulnerability. Limit your compliments, be extremely cautious with physical embraces, ask yourself if someone else should be involved in the counseling along with you, and limit the time spent alone.

There is special advice for ministers of the Gospel when counseling a woman: (1) Consider limiting yourself to a single one-on-one session in the office to assess the need, then apply the Titus 2 principle and find a capable lady to counsel her coupled with your assistance as a consultant. Future sessions should involve the female counselor, if at all possible. (2) When counseling troubled marriages, find positive things to say about the husband's efforts. This will help edify him in the eyes of his wife and deflect attention from you as the model. Undoubtedly, your role as a minister is one of a positive example, but use discernment when comparing yourself to the struggling husband. (3) Keep your leaders informed of any situation that involves counseling a woman, even when it is handled through another lady in the church. (4) As a general principle, discuss your counseling case(s) with the leaders of your church—they may objectively discern a matter or detect potential problems that you may overlook.

Be on guard and take the necessary precautions so that you don't allow your opportunity to minister to become an occasion to sin. Take your direction straight from the Word of God and "let him who thinks he stands take heed that he does not fall" (1 Corinthians 10:12).

TEMPTATION'S SUSCEPTIBLE MOMENTS

Far too many brothers are battling without the necessary weapons. We are in a spiritual battle (1 Corinthians 9:25–27; 2 Corinthians 6:7; 10:4; Ephesians 2:2; 6:11–18) that requires you to be spiritually healthy. Susceptible moments arise when we have been inconsistent spiritually. If you are going to resist the calling of the flesh and the enticements of flirtatious women, you must be equipped spiritually. Men who are equipped spiritually make a consistent commitment to develop as spiritual men of God.

How consistent is your study of God's Word, your prayer life, and your service in the body of Christ? Please do not create false expectations for yourself. Don't for a moment think that reading this book or any other, without a disciplined spiritual life, will provide a solution. No warrior goes to war unequipped. Don't get caught in a susceptible moment asking "where's my sword?" Rather, prepare yourself for the battle through consistently studying God's Word, maintaining a fervent prayer life, and offering yourself in diligent service to God.

HOW TO ESCAPE POTIPHAR'S HOUSE

Life will be full of battles on multiple fronts, and if you do not learn to respond to them, you will become yet another casualty of war. Joseph provides a response that every man would do well to emulate. There are four truths from this biblical episode that will help you win your secret battle.

1. Grasp Human Accountability

Joseph realized he was accountable to Potiphar. So Joseph responded to his wife's persuasions by saying, "You are his wife" (Genesis 39:9). This is a principle of loyalty. Joseph would never be found in the midst of a love triangle. If he was loyal to his Egyptian master, then how much more should we be loyal to our fellow brothers? Scripture has declared that a man who defrauds another brother's bed is worthy of death (see Leviticus 20:10).

2. Accept Personal Responsibility

Joseph realized he was directly responsible. He said, "How then could I do this great evil" (v. 9b). You may be old enough to remember the comic Flip Wilson and his famous saying, "The devil made me do it." It may seem absurd to mention a comic's silly line, but sadly, and far too often, this line is used in a different context to excuse many sinful decisions in society today.

The phrase was designed for humor then but the essence of this infamous line seems to have woven itself into the fabric of society. The world is looking for every reason possible to excuse itself from its responsibility to refrain from violating God's standard. Now homosexuals are claiming that they are born for homosexual expression.[4] Adulterers want to say that they are compelled to find satisfaction elsewhere. There is an industry of excusing a person's actions because he or she is born into a dysfunctional family. Even some Christians claim that the power of Satan tempted them to such an extent that they had to give in to the pressure of suggestion.

A *Dateline NBC* special featured a study to determine the causes for adultery. The scientist who conducted the study concluded that adultery was a part of our genetic makeup, passed on to us millions of years ago. She deduced that cavemen would sleep with other women to increase their clans, and cavewomen would sleep with other men to receive goods. Consequently, this behavior is sown into our genetic makeup. Therefore, it is not totally a person's fault when he or she commits adultery today. The person is simply fulfilling a primal instinct.[5]

This ludicrous thinking finds its way into the church when the blame is placed on a demon of lust, spirit of greed, demon of adultery, etc. If you are to be free, you must accept responsibility for your actions. This is a starting point that God will honor. God's grace for victory does not work in the lives of those who play the victim. I do believe that there are some life experiences that shape a person's thinking, and in turn, may lead to the development of damaging life habits. However, God has made sure that there is always a way of escape (see 1 Corinthians 10:13). It is up to you to take the exit God supplies. Remember, there is lasting victory for those who seek the grace of God. John 8:32–36 assures us that we can walk in the freedom that Christ died to provide for us.

3. Understand Harmartiology

Joseph recognized sin for its true nature—this is the essential definition of harmartiology—understanding the nature of sin. In Genesis 39:9, he referred to the offer of sex as "this great evil." Society renames sin and makes it acceptable. The world describes sin as kleptomania, a phobia, gay, having an affair, alternative lifestyles, and being on the down-low. Sadly, even many in the church do not want to give the violation of God's standard its proper titles—sin, evil, transgression, perversion, and abomination. You may ask, "what is the importance of using the right terms for sin?" It will help you build a biblical grid in your mind that will raise your sensitivity to sin because it is viewed in its proper context. Using humanistic and contemporary terms removes the element of shame, guilt, and disgust that a person should have when engaged in sinful actions.

4. Remember Divine Accountability

Joseph realized that he was divinely accountable. What was the evidence of his divine accountability? When faced with the opportunity to indulge himself in a secret sin, he understood that it really wasn't secret—he knew that it was "against God," who is aware of every human action, desire, and thought. Brother, I must impress upon you that this must be your starting point and your focus. You must live in the reality that in your battle, there is Someone who is always watching.

If you are to think like Joseph (with a sense of divine accountability), you must fear God as he did: "Now Joseph said . . . 'Do this and live, for I fear God'" (Genesis 42:18). I mention this because you may be aware of a person's presence, but if you do not respect their opinion or fear the possibility of their disfavor, it matters little. Fearing God is not a concept that is discussed or taught from many pulpits today, yet it involves the very purpose of man (Proverbs 1:7; Ecclesiastes 12:13). A lack of fear demonstrates man's most profound resistance to God's will (Psalm 36; Romans 3; 1 Peter 2:17). When you are in your secret war, unless you develop a biblical fear of God, the outcome will be what it has been perhaps too often—failure.

Joseph understood the reality of God's presence. According to Genesis 39:11, on this notorious day, Potiphar's wife made her seductive move when, "none of the men of the household was there inside." So why didn't Joseph respond like many other men would have? It is because he knew that he was not truly alone. There was a Divine Presence observing his every move, look, thought, and decision. Wouldn't every man do better in his walk of grace if he could grasp this certainty? Wouldn't men visit fewer porn Web sites? Wouldn't more men protect the honor of their girlfriends or fiancés by waiting until they were married before engaging in sex? Wouldn't fewer violations of the commitment Job made not to gaze on a young woman be registered? (See Job 31:1.)

The answer is obvious. Let's not pretend. If the Savior stood over your shoulder whenever you logged on, you would not visit that site again. If the Savior were standing there when . . . well, you fill in the blank and make the application to your secret war.

In my years in the pastorate, I have observed many occasions when people have adjusted their behavior simply because I entered the room. I suppose I should take some comfort in the fact that I was respected enough that they would not want to continue, but what happens when I leave the room? Is the music turned on again? Do the voices get loud again? Do the touches continue? Is the channel found again? Is the Web page opened again? Give the Lord the respect you give men. Remember, my friend, we serve an omniscient and omnipresent God. Scripture is replete with numerous times when God was watching over His people while they committed evil acts in His sight. For specific examples, see Numbers 32:13; Judges 2:11; 1 Kings 21:6–20; 2 Kings 23:31–37; and 2 Kings 24:8–19. David understood this truth and even asked God the question: "Where can I go from Your Spirit? Or where can I flee from Your presence? If I ascend to heaven, You are there; If I make my bed in Sheol, behold, You are there" (Psalm 139:7–8).

I have never counseled with a person who did not accept the basic truth captured in these verses; however, practicing this theological reality is another matter. You are never beyond God's omnipresent eye. No matter how secret the thought, how secluded the place, how detailed the plans, God is totally aware of your actions and intentions. Practicing an awareness of divine presence kept Joseph from moral failure. Far too many brothers do not practice divine presence because they are not living in everyday presence. Divine presence can only be applied consistently if you are striving for the fellowship of His presence daily. Said another way, do not expect to be sensitive to the Spirit when temptation comes if you have not been nurturing an intimate walk with the Lord in the everyday course of life.

The key to resistance is relationship. Something in your being must love God enough that you are unwilling to offend Him for the temporary pleasure of sin (see Hebrews 11:24–26; John 14:15; Ephesians 4:30). Joseph knew that if he gave in to the passion of his seductress, he would commit an unfaithful act against God. Again, there is wisdom taken from the Word of God for you to consider.

- *"Heal my soul, for I have sinned against You."* (Psalm 41:4)

- *"Against You, You only, I have sinned, and done what is evil in Your sight."* (Psalm 51:4a)

- *"For we have sinned against the Lord."* (Jeremiah 3:25)

- *"I have sinned against heaven."* (Luke 15:21)

Until you deepen your understanding of the fact that yielding to temptation is an unfaithful act against a faithful God, you will have difficulty resisting temptation. Joseph said, "I cannot do this great evil against God." He knew very well whom he would offend!

DEVELOPING A DEFENSE TO WIN YOUR SECRET WAR

If you are a football fan, you have heard it said many times that "a good defense wins championships." For example, the Denver Broncos could never get to the next level until they developed a defense to complement their offensive firepower.

Likewise, winning the war against sexual sins cannot be done without a biblical defense.

CHECK YOUR DISTANCE

If you are going to win your secret battle, you must avoid the places and people who represent seduction (see Genesis 39:10b). Joseph would not expose himself unnecessarily to the woman's seductions. The text says, he would not "be with her." Not only would he not have sex with her, he would eventually flee her presence (v. 12). Why do so many brothers fall to seductresses in various forms? They stay too close to the heat of temptation and eventually get burned. Experience has told me that many victims are attracted to the heat of temptation and think that they can escape in time. However, they soon find themselves caught before they can make an exit. Is this you? There are biblical warnings for those who like the fires of temptation.

For on account of a harlot one is reduced to a loaf of bread, and the adulteress hunts for the precious life. Can a man take fire in his bosom and his clothes not be burned? Or can a man walk on hot coals and his feet not be scorched? So is the one who goes in to his neighbor's wife; whoever touches her will not go unpunished. (Proverbs 6:26–29)

If my heart has been enticed by a woman, or I have lurked at my neighbor's doorway, may my wife grind for another, and let others kneel down over her. For that would be a lustful crime; moreover, it would be an iniquity punishable by judges. For it would be fire that consumes to Abaddon, and would uproot all my increase. (Job 31:9–12)

How many stories do you know of pastors, leaders, husbands, or singles who failed spiritually because they did not take proper precautions? Take the precaution of *flight and pursuit.* Paul said to Timothy, "Flee from youthful lusts." His advice didn't end there; he admonished him to pursue righteousness, faith, love, and peace (2 Timothy 2:22). I make this point to remind you that it is not good enough to flee; you must replace resistance with pursuit. If you remain, temptation will persistently knock until you open the door. Therefore, you must move to another room where the knocks are not heard so clearly. Are you attending movies that create visual or mental voyeurism, surfing the Net without safeties (some need to refrain from surfing altogether), or developing a friendship that should not be? These are all examples of standing within striking distance of spiritual failure. Joseph would not be with the wife of another man. Stop playing with the fires of temptation before you get burned and your house is engulfed in flames!

A man sits in my office with a great sense of guilt and despair in his voice. Why? He initiated a fire that is now burning out of control. It all began with a friendly conversation and ended in intimacy that was only meant for his wife. Now the emotional damage is done, distrust is the norm, and to make matters worse, the children are old enough to discern the tension between Mom and Dad. How will it truly affect them? Only time will tell.

Recently, I was privileged to have Dr. John MacArthur preach a sermon entitled "The Marks of a Man of God" at my installation service. He challenged me and the other men in the congregation to be known for the things we pursue as well as for what we flee from. I had heard this message before on a couple of occasions, but the words resonated, particularly since I was in the midst of writing this chapter. Something tells me that you have read or heard some of the insights I have presented before, but now I ask you to allow them to resonate with you.

Don't treat the truth of the Word with familiarity; always be open to its message. Hebrews 4:12 reminds us that "the word of God is living and active and sharper than any two-edged sword, and piercing as far as the division of soul and spirit, of both joints and marrow, and able to judge the thoughts and intentions of the heart." Never for one moment believe that there is no room for spiritual growth.

CONCLUSION

In the end, the choice is yours to make, my friend. You can live in the bright light of God's holiness (1 Peter 2:19; 1 John 1:7) or flicker in the dark opportunities that the world offers. "Pothipar's wife" is waiting to capture your emotions and lead you or someone you care for on a path of destruction. In all her various forms, she lurks, wanting someone to lie with her. But there is, and there always has been, a way out. Choose it; help others choose it—it is a matter of life and death (James 1:15; 3:13; 5:19–20). No matter how intense the onslaught, the Lord has provided a way of escape (1 Corinthians 10:13).

After a long internal battle of his conscience, a certain man decided that he needed help with the desires that too often led to actions he regretted with each occurrence. But what should he do, to whom should he speak? He asked himself that a hundred times, if not a thousand. Finally, he decided that enough failures had taken place, and he sought the counsel of a mature leader in his church. They began a relationship that involved prayer, radical life choices (which he discovered later weren't so radical), and a great deal of time meditating on the Word and its implications for his life.

With time, this brother gained the victory he had seen so many others rejoice in. He was free from the clutches of fornication. His own personal "Pothiphar's wife" no longer had a stronghold in his life; her allurements had been broken by the grace of God! Now he was a man walking in the freedom that only Christ gives. What changed with him was not a desire for victory; he wanted that from the moment he began traveling the road of sin. The difference was in making the choice to be real and sharing openly with someone else, seeing sin for what it is, and stepping from behind his shell of pseudospirituality to walk in the grace that had been there all the time.

He came to grips with the reality that truly spiritual men are men who recognize their weaknesses and travel the road to wholeness that is only delivered by the Word of God (see John 17:17). My friend, start your journey home today; or help someone else live the life Christ died to provide—choose God. Joseph chose the way of escape and did not listen to her. He did not lie beside her or be with her. Will you?

POINTS OF REFLECTION

1. *Avoid the slippery slopes of Christian liberty*
Compromise takes place when people choose to ignore their distance under the banner of Christian liberty. It seems that for many, this is a false banner of spirituality—an attitude that actually is saying, "I will go as far as I can without sinning." The question you must answer is not how far you can go. The question is: how godly can you be? Many Christian warriors have fallen under the guise of freedom. They seek to remove perimeters and take advantage of their Christian liberty, which for many turns out to be a Christian pitfall. List the areas in which you need to curtail your liberty to avoid sliding down the slippery slope toward committing sexual sins. Be honest and ask yourself if the use of liberty hinders you in becoming a more effective servant for God as described in Galatians 5:13.

2. *Strive for immaturity with the world*
First Corinthians 14:20 instructs us: "Brethren, do not be children in your thinking; yet in evil be infants, but in your thinking be mature." Yes, I'm referring to immaturity when it comes to the subject of evil. It is wise to maintain a child-like experience with the temptations of the world. Men often think they have grown up when they have not. Don't be too familiar with the world's choices, but grow deeper in your walk of faith. What things are you exposing yourself to (entertainment, relationships, etc.) that are questionable from a spiritual standpoint? Ask yourself, "When I make this choice, how spiritual are my thoughts?" Is God pleased with your decision to make the choice to do that certain thing?

3. *Seeking and meditating*

Since the goal of this book is to provide you with biblical solutions to the temptations you face, I will state the obvious —you must seek the wisdom of Scripture.

> *For wisdom will enter your heart and knowledge will be pleasant to your soul; discretion will guard you, understanding will watch over you, to deliver you from the way of evil, from the man who speaks perverse things; from those who leave the paths of uprightness to walk in the ways of darkness; who delight in doing evil and rejoice in the perversity of evil; whose paths are crooked, and who are devious in their ways; to deliver you from the strange woman, from the adulteress who flatters with her words.* (Proverbs 2:10–16)

Notice also the opposite of wisdom and its effects:

> *The woman of folly is boisterous, she is naive and knows nothing. She sits at the doorway of her house, on a seat by the high places of the city, calling to those who pass by, who are making their paths straight: "Whoever is naive, let him turn in here," and to him who lacks understanding she says, "Stolen water is sweet; and bread eaten in secret is pleasant." But he does not know that the dead are there, that her guests are in the depths of Sheol.* (Proverbs 9:13–18)

If you are to resist temptation, you must be armed, and a part of that armor is wisdom. Wisdom is the ability to discern properly, and discernment helps us in our battle against temptation. The word for wisdom carries the connotation of living life with skill. Skill is needed if you are to successfully maneuver through the various inducements that the world places in your path. Collect a list of verses that you can recall when the temptations of the world and the flesh seek to make you stumble. From the verses I have given you and the ones that you find, list ways you can apply them in the course of everyday life. Make every effort to commit yourself to memorizing God's Word—it is the sword of the Spirit and your greatest weapon.

4. *Never forget the cost factor*
There is a price to be paid. Take heed to the strong warning detailed in this biblical account:

> For my husband is not at home, he has gone on a long journey; he has taken a bag of money with him, at the full moon he will come home." With her many persuasions she entices him; with her flattering lips she seduces him. Suddenly he follows her as an ox goes to the slaughter, or as one in fetters to the discipline of a fool, until an arrow pierces through his liver; as a bird hastens to the snare, so he does not know that it will cost him his life. Now therefore, my sons, listen to me, and pay attention to the words of my mouth. Do not let your heart turn aside to her ways, do not stray into her paths. For many are the victims she has cast down, and numerous are all her slain. Her house is the way to Sheol, descending to the chambers of death. (Proverbs 7:19–27)

Taken from Scripture, here are some other considerations before the next temptation presents itself:

- Understand that your spiritual failure grieves the Lord (Ephesians 4:30).

- Be selfless enough to consider that your decision will affect others. Sin never happens in a vacuum; there is always collateral damage—children, your spouse, friends, your testimony (1 Peter 2:11–12).

- Understand that there will be an effect on your future. If you are caught, what will you have to give up?

5. *Get a training partner*

A good training partner is needed for a good workout. He pushes you when you want to call it quits. Make sure you have a partner who will ask you the tough questions and not let you get away with generalities (Proverbs 27:5–6). Be honest, be open, and be consistent in your battle for purity.

LIVING ACCORDING TO THE WILL OF GOD

❶ An Ancient Battle Plan for Purity
1 Thessalonians 4:3–8

— President and Professor Paul Felix

THE harsh reality for Christian men is that we live in a sexually impure world. As one preacher put it, "We live in a culture that sweats sensuality from its pores!"[1] A man today can't escape the temptations that come to him in the sexual realm via television, billboards, magazines, radio programs, and provocatively dressed women. He can run, but he can't hide. The world he lives in is saturated with sexual temptations and sexual sins.

What's a man to do? More particularly, what is an African American Christian man to do to prevent the sensual steam of the culture from spraying his life and leaving him dirty? Today's generation of African American men is not the first one to live in a sex-crazed culture. A journey back to the times of the New Testament reveals that the cultures of the cities of Corinth and Thessalonica also sweated sensuality from their pores.

What made these cities worse than ours today is that they were pagan to the core. These cities had no history of being influenced by the Gospel of the Lord Jesus Christ prior to the apostle Paul proclaiming it to them. Corinth and Thessalonica did not have the privilege of having people in their midst who knew the true and living God like the cities of America today. These ancient cities were dominated by a perspective toward sex that left God out. Yet when the Gospel came to those places, the Christians were expected to be sexually pure. In fact, they were commanded by the Word of God to avoid sexual sin (1 Corinthians 6:12–20; 1 Thessalonians 4:3–8). It was a radical call, but one that was consistent with the Gospel.

The Bible proclaims that Christian men are called to live pure lives at all times. Although the Christian African American male is bombarded with the lure to sin sexually, he must remember that sexual purity is God's standard for him! In order to achieve the standard, brothers must stand on the will of God as found in the Word of God. They must follow the strategy found in the Bible. The battle plan for purity is not new. It is an ancient one that is applicable to all Christian men who seek to please God in the area of their sexuality.

Paul's letter to the young believers who lived in the sex-saturated city of Thessalonica provides the ancient battle plan for how a brother can be pure in a dirty world. First, he must recapture a biblical view of sexual purity. Next, he must rely upon the biblical guidelines for sexual purity. Finally, he must remember the biblical motivating reasons for sexual purity.

RECAPTURE A PROPER
VIEW OF SEXUAL PURITY

The battle plan for a sexually pure life requires an attitude adjustment. Our perspective on purity has to be revamped so that it reflects God's outlook and not that of the world. The world's perspective on sexual purity is obvious. The fact that sexual sin is rampant speaks volumes about what the world thinks about purity as it relates to sexuality. The world has kicked sexual purity to the curb. It has taken the concept of sanctifying one's sexuality and thrown it into the garbage dump. It views sexual purity as an old and archaic idea that has no relevance for present-day living.

Because of this sad fact, the African American man who desires to make a commitment to sexual purity must renew his mind with the truth of Scripture regarding this subject. Paul's writing in Romans 12:2 supports the fact that there must be a continual renewal of the mind so that man will see purity from God's vantage point and not from the one that was formed during his developmental years. Manhood is often presented to the young African American male in terms of one's sexual prowess and ability. During the formative years of his life, it is etched in his mind that to be a "man" is determined by how many sexual encounters he has. If he doesn't meet the standards in this area, it is hinted that perhaps he has homosexual tendencies.

This type of thinking is reinforced by the TV shows that he watches, the music he listens to, the material that he reads, and his observation of the lifestyle of the brothers around him. A steady dose of viewing music videos on BET in the late evening and early morning will shape his mind to believe that women are no more than sexual objects to be admired for their ability to shake their behinds. The latest

R&B songs will have him humming and singing words about sex that are contrary to the teachings of Scripture. J. Holiday's "Bed," Gucci Mane's "Freaky Gurl," and Beyoncé's "Get Me Bodied" will warp his understanding of sexual purity. The lyrics of James Brown's "Sex Machine" and Billy Paul's "Me and Mrs. Jones" have also distorted the thinking of many African American men.

Brothers must rid themselves of this thinking that comes from the gutter of the world. Instead, it is imperative that their thoughts concerning sexual purity reflect the glorious view of heaven. The opening words of the apostle Paul in 1 Thessalonians 4:3 are designed to give the Thessalonians a proper perspective of sexual purity. Paul writes, "For this is the will of God, your sanctification; that is, that you abstain from sexual immorality." What becomes clear from these opening words is that a person's sexuality cannot be divorced from his sanctification. The apostle will not allow his readers to drive a wedge between holiness and sexuality. He will not permit the Christian to treat his sanctification and his sexuality as if they belong to two different worlds. The two are not to be isolated, but integrated.

There were some in the Corinthian church who thought that sexuality and sanctification had nothing to do with each other. They had a little saying, "Food for the body and the body for food," that they also adapted for sex. "Sex for the body and the body for sex" is how some of the Corinthians thought. The apostle Paul corrects their improper thinking by saying, "Yet the body is not for immorality, but for the Lord, and the Lord is for the body" (1 Corinthians 6:13b).

It is possible that the Thessalonians thought that sex was no big deal. They may have simply seen it as a bodily function. Regardless of how they once viewed their sexuality,

Paul wants their minds to be renewed so that they see their sexuality as God does.

How does Paul revamp the view of the Thessalonians so that they have a proper perspective on sexual purity? He does it by pointing out that the command to abstain from sexual immorality does not stand in isolation. Rather, this command is linked to sanctification, which is linked to God's will, which is linked to walking in obedience to God and pleasing Him. You see, the believer's sexuality is part of a chain that is ultimately related to living for God and pleasing Him (see figure 1). This puts sexual purity in its proper context and connects it to the glory of heaven.

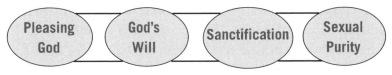

Figure 1

Let me establish the chain for you. The first link in the chain is identified in 4:1–2. Here Paul reminds the Thessalonians that when he was with them, he instructed them as to how they ought to walk and please God. His heart's desire was that they live in such a way that God would be satisfied. After Paul left the Thessalonians, he received various reports which indicated that the Thessalonians had heeded his exhortation. The apostle could then write that they were actually pleasing God in their walk. This does not mean that they were perfect in every respect. Paul's request and exhortation that they excel still more in their walk indicates there was still room for spiritual growth.

The apostle continues the chain by relating the second link, God's will, to the first link, walking and pleasing God.

He understands that if a Christian is to please God, then he must know the will of God. It is impossible to please almighty God without knowing His will. Paul introduces the Thessalonians to the will of God by simply stating, "This is the will of God." A more literal, but a specific rendering would be "this is a will of God." The meaning of Paul's words is not that this is the only will of God or that this is the complete will of God, but simply that this is an aspect of God's will. Later in this epistle, the apostle will say that rejoicing always, praying without ceasing, and giving thanks in everything are also components of God's will (1 Thessalonians 5:16–18).

The phrase "your sanctification" identifies the third link in the chain that starts with walking and pleasing God and ends with sexual purity. The apostle links sanctification to God's will. This phrase zeroes in on the particular aspect of God's will that Paul wants the readers to excel in. At this point in his epistle, Paul is not concerned with the whole will of God for the Thessalonians. Rather, what is uppermost in his mind is the part of God's will that is specifically related to their sanctification.

The word *sanctification* and its related forms are used several times in 1 Thessalonians (3:13; 4:7; 5:23). There are two basic ideas involved in this word: separation and devotion. The will of God for the believer is that he must be separated from sin and that he also be devoted to God. This is the explicit will of God for the child of God.

The apostle Peter declares this same message to the people of God who were sojourners scattered throughout Pontus, Galatia, Cappadocia, Asia, and Bithynia. In his first letter that bears his name, Peter writes, "But like the Holy One who called you, be holy yourselves also in all your behavior" (1 Peter 1:15). These Christians are commanded to be holy. They are informed that the standard for their holy living is God Himself. Also, they are told that holiness is to touch every area of their behavior. No part of the Christian's life is to be untouched or unaffected by holiness. In essence, Peter writes that the believer's words, thoughts, and actions are to be marked by holiness.

The fourth and final link in this chain is abstaining from sexual immorality. Sanctification is to be applied to every area of the believer's walk and talk. Yet Paul does not focus on universal holiness as Peter does. His concern is how sanctification relates to a particular area of the lives of the Thessalonians. Holy living (sanctification) for these believers means that they "abstain from sexual immorality."

The proper perspective on abstaining from sexual immorality is to see it within the context of living a holy life. Living a life of holiness, that is, sanctification, is crucial because it is part of God's will for the believer. It is critical to know God's will if the child of God is going to walk and please God. Sexual purity matters to God. That is the view that must be recaptured. A failure to have God's perspective on refraining from sexual sin will cripple the walk of the African American Christian male who seeks to be pure.

RELY UPON THE GUIDELINES FOR SEXUAL PURITY

The ancient battle plan for sexual purity that the apostle Paul offers to the African American Christian male is not only concerned with a proper view of sexual purity, but also with the practice of sexual purity. Brothers, it is admirable to view your sexuality from the viewpoint of God and His Word. Yet, if this Scripture-informed perspective does not lead to the practice of holy living in the area of sex, then you have abandoned the biblical strategy for winning the secret sex wars. It is not enough to recapture a proper view of sexual purity. You must go a step further and rely upon the guidelines for living a life that is free from any trace of immorality as Paul warns in Ephesians 5:3. Correct thinking about true sexual morality must result in the implementation of the biblical principles for being sexually clean.

In 1 Thessalonians 4:3b-6, the apostle Paul gives instruction and a reminder on how to live a pure life in an impure world. The text gets down to where the rubber meets the road and gives a threefold course of action that will result in the believer's sexuality being purified by holiness.

The first guideline for sexual purity is: avoid sexual sin (4:3b). Men, if you are going to win the battle for sexual purity, then it begins with the concerted effort to stay away from sexual sin. Sexual sin is to be avoided like a deadly plague. Hear Paul, and hear him well, when he says at the end of verse 3, "that you abstain from sexual immorality." This phrase serves a dual purpose. As was mentioned earlier, it defines what sanctification means for the Thessalonians. Sanctification for the Thessalonians means sexual purity. At the same time, it also commands them to have nothing at all to do with sexual immorality. The word *abstain* means "to keep away," "to hold oneself off of," and "to be distant." It is a term that fits very nicely with the idea of sanctification because both words are stressing the idea of separation.

The thing that the Thessalonians are to distance themselves from is "sexual immorality." Depending on what Bible you read, the Greek word that Paul uses is translated "sexual immorality," "fornication," "sexual sins," "unchastity," or even "whoredom." The term refers to any type of unlawful sexual activity as established by the Word of

God. There are a number of sexual sins that fall under the umbrella of this term. Premarital sex, extramarital sex, pornography, incest, bestiality, and even masturbation would be included in this term.[2]

The believer must separate himself from sexual immorality. He must distance himself from sexual sin. He is to keep himself as far away as possible from sexual immorality so that there is not even a trace of it in his life. There should not even be a hint of the smell of impurity when it comes to the Christian's life. This is the essence of what the apostle Paul tells the believers at Ephesus: "But immorality or any impurity or greed must not even be named among you, as is proper among saints" (Ephesians 5:3).

Abstain from sexual immorality. Do not entertain it! Flee from sexual sin. Do not flirt with it! Distance yourself from fornication. Do not delight in it! Isolate yourself from all unlawful sexual activities. Don't integrate them into your life! Men, these are not clever little sayings that you are being given. Instead, these are gentle rebukes, which call you to abandon the world's standards and to cleave to God's standards.

The tragedy is that there are African American Christian men who do not maintain a great distance between themselves and sexual sin. There are brothers who flirt with sexual sin, who delight in sensuality, and who have integrated unlawful sexual activities into their life. Yet the guideline is to avoid, to distance, to flee, to separate, and to abstain from any unlawful sexual activity. Proverbs 6:27 asks a profound question, "Can a man take fire to his bosom, and his clothes not get burned?" It suggests that the closer you get to sexual sin, the greater the danger is for you to be burned by it. Don't look at TV shows that promote sensuality. Avoid listening to music that will fill your mind with impure thoughts. Turn your eyes away from looking at women who dress in tantalizing ways.

The second guideline for sexual purity is: control your body (1 Thessalonians 4:4–5). The mastery of one's body is crucial to the achievement of sexual purity. Men, we will never, ever win the battle for sexual purity unless we bring our sexual desires under the lordship of Christ. Having no control over your body means there will be an absence of sexual purity. Listen to Paul's words in verse 4. He writes, "[For this is the will of God] . . . that each of you know how to possess his own vessel in sanctification and honor."

The opening words of verse four have been, and are, an interpretive battlefield. Much has been written about what Paul means when he says, "to possess his own vessel." One camp says it means "to acquire a wife." The other camp says it means "to control your body." The writer takes the position that it means "to control your body."[3]

The apostle Paul looks his readers right in the eyes and tells them that if they want to be sexually pure, then each one of them must know how to control his body. He is not looking at his readers as a crowd, but as individuals. He says, "each of you." This guideline is given to individuals and not to the group collectively. Each one of them must "know how" to possess his body. The phrase "know how" suggests that learning is involved. The implication is that this knowledge does not come automatically. Through the process of experience, the believer learns how to keep his body in check. He has learned that if he exposes his body to certain temptations, he is flirting with danger. Therefore, like the apostle Paul wrote in 1 Corinthians 9:27, a wise man buffets his body and makes it his slave.

When it comes to controlling the body, there are two options. The body can be controlled in a godly way or in an ungodly way. Obviously, if a person is going to be sexually pure it is required that he control his body in a godly way. Paul spells out what this means in the last part of verse 4, when he says, "in sanctification and honor." The believer's body should be controlled to the extent that it falls within the realm of "sanctification." In other words, he should discipline his body so that it is marked by separation from sin and devotion to God. The believer's body must also be controlled to the extent that it falls within the realm of honor. The Thessalonians were obligated to treat their bodies with honor. They were to handle themselves in such a way that it brought glory to God and to Christ. It matters what a believer does with his body. The body of the Christian is the temple of the Holy Spirit, and he should treat it that way.

The body can also be controlled in an ungodly way. A believer who controls his body in this way is guilty of not exercising any restraint at all. He does what comes naturally. He acts "like the Gentiles who do not know God" by allowing his "lustful passion" to dominate him as Paul noted in 1 Thessalonians 4:5. Lust-produced passions dictate what he will do when it comes to his sexuality. If he gets the urge, he'll do it. If it feels good, then he will have it his way. This person is very much like a dog that acts on instinct. It is natural for sinners to be led by the passions that are associated with not knowing Jesus Christ as Lord. Believers are not to be driven by the passion of lust, but rather by a passion for purity.

Men, control your bodies! But make sure you control your bodies in a manner that is holy and honorable and not in a way that is characteristic of those who are unsaved.

The third guideline for sexual purity is: don't sin against your brother (4:6a). The African American believing male who is serious about practicing sexual purity must conduct himself in such a way that he does not sin against his Christian brother or sister. Whether he realizes it or not, sexual immorality is not only a sin against God and one's own body as Paul points out in 1 Corinthians 6:18—but it is also a sin against another individual.

The biblical character Joseph understood this principle. When he was tempted by Potiphar's wife to commit sin with her, one of the guidelines that enabled him to say no to this temptation was his understanding that she was Potiphar's wife. He told her, "You are his wife." Joseph saw sexual sin not only as a great evil, but also as a sin against another individual.

The apostle Paul drives this principle home to the Thessalonians in the first part of verse 6 when he writes, "and that no man transgress and defraud his brother in the matter." The phrase, "in the matter," is not a reference to a new topic of business dealings, as some would suggest. That is foreign to the context of this verse. Rather, it refers to the matter of avoiding sexual immorality. It refers to sanctification as it relates to sexual purity. In this matter, the believer is not to transgress and defraud his brother.

The concern is sinning against one's "brother." The word *brother* is to be understood in the same sense that it has been throughout this epistle. It refers to fellow members of the body of Christ, both male and female. Paul begins this chapter by saying, "Finally, then, brethren." It is clear that he is addressing both the brothers and the sisters of the congregation. Therefore, the concern is that the Thessalonians avoid sinning against another Christian sexually.

To *transgress* one's brother or sister in the sexual area is to go beyond the boundaries that God has established in His Word. Sexual sin is a going beyond, a stepping over the line that God has established as it relates to another individual. The young man who is involved in premarital sex has crossed over the line that has been established by God in his relationship with that young woman. The man who is involved in extramarital sex has gone beyond the limits that God has established for him in his relationship with another woman. A guideline for sexual purity is to not transgress a fellow believer in the matter of sex. In other words, view the other believer as having a sign around his or her neck that says, "Do not trespass." When it comes to relationships, don't go beyond what the Word of God says is proper and permissible.

To *defraud* one's brother or sister in the sexual area is to take advantage of the individual when it comes to sexual matters. Paul also uses the phrase "take advantage of" in 2 Corinthians. In that epistle, Paul states that neither he nor Titus took advantage of the Corinthians (7:2; 12:17–18). He also mentions that it is Satan's desire to take advantage of the believer (2:11). A man must not act like Satan and take advantage of other believers when it comes to sexual matters. He must avoid defrauding his brothers and sisters, cheating them, or swindling them in any way.

Every act of sexual sin must be seen for what it really is—it is an act of taking advantage of another individual either directly or indirectly. When a teenaged male has premarital sex with a young girl for the first time, he has defrauded not only her, but also her future husband. When a believer masturbates while fantasizing about a woman, he has cheated that woman and used her in a way that violates her and her mate.

I pray that you will put into practice the guideline of not sinning against another Christian. Allow it to guide your actions as you seek to follow the biblical strategy for sexual purity.

REMEMBER THE MOTIVATING
REASONS FOR SEXUAL PURITY

Paul concludes his discussion of the battle plan for sexual purity by turning his attention to some compelling reasons for being pure in an impure world. The motivating reasons for sexual purity that he offers are different from what brothers often hear today. African American men are told to avoid sexual sin because of the risk of venereal diseases. They are challenged to "wrap it up" so that they might not catch AIDS. They are encouraged to limit their sexual activity in light of the high number of babies born out of wedlock. These may be practical reasons, but they are not the biblical ones that are offered in Scripture.

Why should the African American Christian man recapture a proper view of sexual purity? Why should he follow the guidelines for living a holy life when it comes to his sexuality? The first reason is that sexual sin will be repaid by God (1 Thessalonians 4:6b). Jesus Christ does not take sexual sin lightly! The Lord of the church and the One through whom God will judge all men does not have a "lite" view of sexual sin.

Paul wants the Thessalonians to know that when it comes to sexual immorality, "the Lord is *the* avenger in all these things." Yes, Jesus Christ loves them with an everlasting love. He has forgiven all of their sins, past, present, and future. But when it comes to deterring sexual sin in their lives, the apostle wants them to have a picture hanging on the wall of their minds of Jesus as the avenger. He is the One who takes it upon Himself to punish those who fail to follow God's will regarding their sexuality. The contemporary Christian may not like this image of Jesus Christ. Yet it is a portrait of Christ that is presented in God's Word. And it is presented to cause believers to abstain from sexual immorality.

The apostle does not give the specifics concerning how God will repay, but only that He *will* repay! This teaching of Paul is consistent with the warning the writer of Hebrews gives when he exhorts his readers to keep the marriage bed undefiled. He cautions in Hebrews 13:4, "For fornicators and adulterers God will judge."

The message that God will punish sexual sin was not a new message to the Thessalonians. This warning to them was in harmony with the previous teaching that the missionaries had imparted when they were with them ("just as we also told you before"). Yet Paul and his companions didn't just tell them that Jesus will repay sexual sin; they also earnestly testified that Jesus Christ is the avenger when it comes to sexual immorality.

A second motivating reason for proper behavior in the sexual realm is that sexual sin is incompatible with God's calling (4:7). The Thessalonians are reminded that when God calls a person to salvation, the purpose or goal of that call is not for sensuality. Paul writes, "For God has not called us for the purpose of impurity." The Christians at Thessalonica were not saved in order to be involved in sexual filth or dirt. Rather, in stark contrast, the Thessalonians are told that their call to salvation was rooted and grounded in sanctification and is to result in holiness in every area of life. God didn't call them to be impure. But when God did call them to salvation, it was a call that was planted in the soil of holiness and was to result in a life that bloomed with the petals of purity.

A final reason that should compel the African American Christian man to a lifestyle of purity is that sexual sin is a rejection of God and His gift (4:8). Paul concludes his teaching on the necessity to sanctify their sexuality by informing the Thessalonians that a person who rejects the biblical teaching on sexual purity is not rejecting the teacher (in this case the apostle Paul) or some other person. Instead, this individual is rejecting God!

Sexual purity is the standard that God Himself has set for His people. The preachers and teachers of sexual purity are simply instruments that God uses to get His standard across to them. Therefore, a person who does not abstain from sexual immorality and who does not control his body in a holy and honorable way is not rejecting the messenger, but God. Such an individual raises his fist and shakes it in the face of God. He defies God! He rebels against almighty God and not some puny man.

Sexual sin is also a rejection of God's gift. God is identified as the One who gives His Holy Spirit to the believer. What an amazing gift the believer has received. At the point of salvation, the Spirit of God, who is described as holy, is given to the believer so that the believer can be holy in God's sight. It needs to be remembered that the third person of the Trinity is the Spirit of God, who is the Holy Spirit. When a man is involved in sexual sin, he is rejecting God and the gift God has given him to make him holy.

Sexual sin will be repaid by the Lord Jesus Christ. It is incompatible with God's calling and a rejection of God and His gift. Brothers, these are compelling and motivating reasons to pursue sexual purity! May these reasons become the convictions of your heart so that you can say, like Joseph when tempted with sexual sin, "How then could I do this great evil and sin against God!" (Genesis 39:9b).

CONCLUSION

Sexual sin is destroying individuals, marriages, families, churches, and communities. Sex before marriage (fornication), sex outside of marriage (adultery), sex with members of the same sex (homosexuality), and sex with oneself (masturbation) are having a devastating impact upon African Americans. Many African American Christian men are losing their secret sex wars. Some are casualties of the wars. Others fail as they seek to win the wars. The good news is that the believer in Jesus Christ can win the battle for sexual purity.

The battle plan for sexual purity comes to us from the early church, but it is relevant. The strategy calls for African American Christian men to recapture a proper view of sexual purity (1 Thessalonians 4:3a), to rely upon the guidelines for sexual purity (4:3b–6a), and to remember the motivating reasons for sexual purity (4:6b–8). This ancient plan that is rooted in the Word of God will enable God's men of color to win the war for purity.

Brothers, the battle is fierce and intense, but with the help of God and His Word, it can be won. May you experience the freedom from sexual sin that is yours in Jesus Christ!

POINTS OF REFLECTION

1. In order to recapture a proper view of sexual purity, your mind needs to be continually renewed with the Word of God. Identify what the following Scriptures teach about sexual purity: Genesis 2:24; Proverbs 5:18; 1 Corinthians 6:18; Ephesians 5:3; Colossians 3:5; Hebrews 13:4. Memorize at least two of these verses and be diligent about obeying God's Word.

2. The strategy for sexual purity demands that you distance yourself from sexual immorality. What are some sexual sins that you are getting too close to? What specific activity or circumstance is causing you to get too close to that particular sin? Make a commitment to radically deal with those things that are bringing you too close to sexual sin (Matthew 5:27–30; 1 Corinthians 6:18; Colossians 3:5).

3. The battle plan laid out in God's Word will prepare you for a pure life; it requires that you control your body. Read Psalm 139:23–24 and ask God to search your heart so that you will be able to determine where you fall short in buffeting your body. Share with a godly friend your struggles in controlling your body. Request that he will intercede on your behalf so that you might gain mastery of your body.

4. Three motivating reasons for sexual purity were given. Which one are you most likely to forget when you are tempted with sexual sin? Memorize this motivating reason and also the Scripture that it is based upon.

5. Each and every day you should pray for your purity. Review this chapter and develop a list of seven items that you need to pray about. Use the seven days of the week to pray for one item each day. You should continue doing this until God answers your prayers.

LEARNING FROM MEN WHO HAVE FALLEN

A Flawed Battle Plan to Avoid
2 Samuel 11

— Pastor Robert S. Scott Sr.

THERE she was, looking right at me, seductive and inviting. I was all alone in the back of a coworker's delivery van. He had called in sick that day and I was assigned to do his route. And there she posed (quite a famous celebrity, at that) on the cover of a popular porn magazine, enticing me to look at her.

What would you do? That was over ten years ago and I can still remember that day. I remember it so well because all day long I was tempted to compromise my purity. In the privacy of a closed cabin, I could have sat down and satisfied my lust. I was being tempted to believe the lie that yielding to sexual temptation isn't a problem if you can keep it a secret. But on that day I didn't believe that lie. I didn't sin. I turned the magazine over and covered it up with a supply box. Instead of lusting, I rejoiced because by God's grace, I had won that battle.

For years in my life, I would not have thought twice about savoring every page of that magazine. I was exposed to pornography and sexual immorality at a young age, as perhaps you were. Sexual sin ruled my life with an iron rod. The motto that all of my friends and I had lived by was "Get all the girls, glory, and gold you can get." That was my pursuit, that is, until Jesus saved me and changed me. Some twenty-three years ago, Jesus set me free from my enslavement to sexual immorality, and He empowered me to battle against sexual temptations instead of passively yielding to them.

Can you relate to my story? Did it cause you to think back to a time when you were tempted in much the same way by a magazine on a newsstand, an adult video in the local video store, a provocative pop-up on the computer screen? Was it ten years ago, a year ago? Or maybe it was last month, last week, or even yesterday? If you can answer yes to any of these questions, and if you are battling to resist the seemingly everywhere-present lure of sexual temptation, then, brother, let me assure you that you are not alone.

I have served in pastoral ministry for about twenty years, and I don't know of a class of men anywhere who do not have to fight to live a life of purity. Older men have to battle as well as the young, mature believers as well as new believers, pastors in the pulpit as well as parishioners in the pew, brothers who read books on purity as well as brothers who write them. The key to maintaining a consistent life of purity is not the presence or absence of the battle. Everyone is in the battle. The key is how you do battle. So let me be clear that if you intend to live a life of purity, you will have to resolve to battle for purity every day for the rest of your life.

I have taken the subject of this chapter from the life of one of the godliest men in the Bible to demonstrate to you that no one is exempt from this struggle. He is so revered that Acts 13:22 states that God referred to him as "A MAN AFTER MY HEART, who will do all My will." Yet, in the darkest episode of his life, he was tempted by sexual sin, followed a deceptively flawed battle plan, and succumbed to his temptation. This account of David is described in 2 Samuel 11.

Brothers, I need you to stay with me. If you are going to win your secret sex wars, then you must get your arms around two critically important points. One, if godly King David struggled and fell, both you and I need to make sure that we learn from his failure so that when we are tempted, we don't fall. And second, we need to make sure that we follow a biblical battle plan, which will empower us to consistently live a life of purity.

UNDISCIPLINED LEISURE TIME
WILL LEAD TO MORAL FAILURE

"Then *it* happened in the spring, at the time when *kings* go out to battle, that David sent Joab and his servants with him and all Israel" (2 Samuel 11:1). The pronoun *it* in this verse refers to the most disastrous episode in David's life, and *it* didn't happen to David while he was on the battlefield. Instead, David experienced the battle of his life in the privacy of his own home.

The danger arose so subtly that it seems almost imperceptible in the text. Did you notice that the Bible states that "at the time when *kings* go out to battle" *King* David stayed home? The Word of God emphasizes that every able, qualified male went to the battlefield but David. The next verse exposes the problem more clearly. It states, "When evening came David arose from his bed" (verse 2). Evening is the time between sunset and nightfall. Do you get the picture? While all the men of Israel were fighting for the Lord on the battlefield, King David didn't just stay at home. King David stayed in bed until late afternoon. Herein lies the first lesson in avoiding moral failure: The destructive path toward sexual immorality begins as subtly as using leisure time in undisciplined ways.

The fact that David chose to stay home and relax didn't mean that he was no longer in a battle. We have an external enemy who is not flesh and blood (Satan) and an internal enemy that we must kill daily (sin). So we can never assume that it is safe to take undisciplined leisure time. We are always at war because our Enemy is always lurking to devour us. Even more sobering is the fact that Satan has breached our borders, invading our culture and even our homes. He has poisoned many of our sources of leisure. There is no place where we can relax without the threat of attack. Therefore, we must be on the alert at all times. In the battle for purity, we must start fighting the battle where it begins. It is okay to take leisure time, but we must stay vigilant and diligently guard how we use it (2 Timothy 1:7; 2:3–4).

LOOKING WILL LEAD TO MORAL FAILURE

Because King David chose to use his leisure time in an undisciplined way, he stumbled into a very dangerous battle. Second Samuel 11:2 casually states that David walked onto his roof and "saw a woman bathing; and the woman was *very beautiful* in appearance." Now he wasn't using his R&R time looking for the "kind of girl you can't bring home to mamma," nor was he carousing with pagan women in some nightclub or pagan strip joint. He wasn't even doing what many of us do, surfing the channels, when all of a sudden—bam!—a nude scene pops onto our HDTV screen. He was just relaxing, minding his own business, and there she was—a beautiful, nude woman.

This is precisely the danger I am warning against that can occur with the undisciplined use of your leisure time. You make yourself vulnerable to seeing things that you shouldn't look at (whether on TV, the Internet, or wherever). Now before you cast stones at beautiful Bath(ing)-sheba, you should know that it was perfectly normal to bathe on one's roof. Unlike our Hollywood starlets today who clamor for attention, she may not have known that she had an audience. Both David and Bathsheba could have been simply trying to escape the heat of a sweltering spring day.

The problem was that David's roof was higher than hers, and she started bathing before it was dark enough to conceal her body, so he got an eyeful. That left him with a tough question to answer. "Is it a sin to keep looking at a nude woman's body?" Brothers, you have to answer this question right. Why? Because in today's porn-filled world, you can be sure that at some place and in some way, you too will either intentionally, unwittingly, or innocently be exposed to a "Bathsheba."

I'll tell you up front that David didn't answer that question right. By today's standard he looked at what could be considered a PG-13 rated movie (this rating contains nonsexual nudity, sensuality). In the following paragraphs, let me give you a biblical battle plan that will help you win your war against the enticing temptation of pornography.[1]

Avoid Pornography—It Is Sin

You may have heard it said, or perhaps even used this line yourself to justify checking someone out, "You can look, so long as you don't touch." Brothers, that doesn't come from God. That is a lie straight from the mouth of Satan. The Bible repeatedly warns us that looking can be a grave sin, in and of itself. Jesus declared, "But I say to you that everyone who *looks* at a woman with lust for her has already committed adultery with her in his heart" (Matthew 5:28). Jesus explains that looking is the firstfruits that sprout from a heart rooted in lust. Solomon warns also, "Do not desire her beauty in your heart, nor let her capture you with her eyelids. For on account of a harlot *one is reduced* to a loaf of bread, and an adulteress hunts for the precious life" (Proverbs 6:25–26).

God made women beautiful, and He also hardwired men to appreciate that beauty. It's foolish to pretend that it's no big deal when "Ms. All That" pops onto your screen, walks into view, or wiggles on a commercial. The question is: is it okay to look at nude women who are being provocative, or not? Let's allow the Bible to answer that question.

Avoid Pornography—It Is Perverting

On one hand, in creating women in His image and likeness (Genesis 1:26–27), God intends for men to view women with all the dignity proper for a person who reflects and represents the likeness of our invisible God. On the other hand, in creating clothing (Genesis 3:21), God doesn't intend for men to look at naked women at our own discretion. Just like Adam and Eve's fig leaves didn't cover enough, the clothes that men and women make today often don't either. The word used for garments in verse 21 suggests that God made tunics or long (non-sheer, non-body-hugging) robes to wear.[2] God did this because when sin entered the world, it took up residence in all of our hearts (Mark 7:21–23).

As sinners, our lust easily perverts the God-given, powerful passion to reproduce and multiply. Lust enslaves us to an insatiable desire for sex even when this means obtaining sex outside of the bounds of His holy will. In response to that issue, God instituted clothing in order to protect and preserve His special gift, which is the enjoyment of nudity for private moments between a married man and his wife.

Outside of that God-blessed union, looking at nakedness perverts us in two ways. First, looking at nudity allows our strong passion for sex to dominate us. It takes precedence in our hearts, even over our desire to please God.[3] Second, pornography perverts our appreciation of women so that we feel justified in looking at *all* women (even those who are not intentionally trying to be immodest) as objects rather than honoring them as divine image-bearers. The Word of God specifically charges us not to do that.

The apostle Paul exhorted Timothy to relate to "the younger women [in the church] as sisters, in all purity" (1 Timothy 5:2). That means you must learn to treat your sisters with a dignity that honors women; they are not to be treated like objects to be had. So, brothers, choose wisely whose ways you will follow. God made clothing as a covering so that you can keep your focus on Him. Satan wants to expose women to defile and pervert your passions. If you are going to win your secret sex wars, then you have to follow God's marching orders and stop yielding to Satan.

Avoid Pornography—It Is a Dangerous Snare

There is a common saying which suggests that "a little peek won't hurt." If you believe that, there are many movies, porn producers, and women who will give you a whole lot to peek at. Here again, the Bible is not silent, brothers. The Word of God exhorts us to discipline our minds and regard immodest women as different from our modest sisters. Solomon instructs: "As a ring of gold in a swine's snout so is a beautiful woman who lacks discretion" (Proverbs 11:22). This means that instead of lusting over immodest, seductive women, you must view them like ornaments intentionally displayed in a grotesque way.

Be convinced, brothers, since God said this, He will enable you to do it. You can overcome the temptation to peek at scantily dressed and nude women by knowing that they are not eye candy, but rather soul poison. Also, know that if you don't discipline your mind to think of them biblically, as dangerous goods, Proverbs 7:24–27 warns that immodest women will ensnare you in a deadly trap. If the truth be told and our secret sex wars exposed, we'd find that there are far too many brothers stuck in that trap.

Avoid Pornography—It Is Committing Visual Fornication or Adultery

Perhaps the clincher in flawed thinking is that in order to justify looking at what we know we shouldn't look at, we tell ourselves that "it's only looking." That type of thinking comes from allowing our sinful desires to govern our thoughts. At that point we are embracing a Hugh Hefner-like pagan worldview, which excuses and even promotes looking at nude women.[4] But brothers, God is the Master Architect who fashioned all the shapes and curves of a woman's nude body. Therefore, He alone is the One who determines if only looking *really* is only looking and if that is okay.

To that point the Bible explicitly teaches that you cannot

separate those two acts. Jesus made it real plain. He equated looking with lust to committing adultery (Matthew 5:27). Therefore, know that when you choose to look at women pornographically, you train your mind to believe Satan's lie and to deny God's truth that you have taken the first step in committing sexual sin. At this point you've bitten the hook and can't free yourself as you might have thought. God placed within us powerful sexual urges, which when aroused, burst forth and drive us with a desire to complete the act.

That is why most men who watch pornography also masturbate. Pornography is like a gateway drug.[5] It leads you down a slippery slope into all sorts of other perversions of God's ideal purpose for sex. Brothers, don't be deceived. Looking at pornography isn't only looking. It is engaging in visual and illicit sex, which often leads to a desire to fulfill inflamed, unsanctioned passions.

Avoid Pornography—It Distorts Our View of God and His Gift of Sex

Another self-destructive, flawed way of thinking about sex is that it is okay to look at women to whom you are not married. Celebrating celibacy for singles, monogamy for married couples, and heterosexual marriages seems a bit outdated in our age of tolerance—even among some professing Christians. Brothers, there can only be one individual behind a campaign to portray biblical views as outdated and prudish —Satan. He markets lies in order to get you to put down the one weapon that you can use to defeat him—your Sword.

Satan wants you to forego your commitment to follow God's ways so that he can lure you into following his road to destruction. He does this by painting a false caricature of God as an old sexual scrooge, and then he promotes himself as the hero who brings us "the good life." You have to see through these lies and know that nothing Satan promotes as good is actually good. Remember, he is the one who told Eve that eating from the wrong tree was a good thing to do.

The so-called good life that he promotes is a slippery slope that leads to deeper sin. He tries to lure you in with visual promiscuity (pornography), arouse you with audio promiscuity (phone sex), enslave you with physical indulgence (fornication and adultery), and destroy you with dangerous and illegal sex. Having a clear biblical direction is the only way to guard yourself against the schemes of the Devil.

In contradiction to his lies about the Word of God, the Bible openly affirms that God's purpose for nudity is to give exhilarating joy through marital sex (Proverbs 5:18–19). God, who created everything seen and unseen, didn't declare that His creation was "very good" until He finished shaping a very beautiful, curvaceous woman. Then God brought a naked, very good-looking Eve to her mate, Adam. He joined them in holy matrimony and blessed them to enjoy a *one flesh* sexual union (Genesis 2:21–24). God considered that act to be perfectly good and innocent because Genesis 2:25 proclaims, "And the man and his wife were both naked and were not ashamed." It is clear from Scripture that God blesses couples who passionately enjoy their nudity within a marriage union (Song of Solomon 4:10–5:1). God is the giver of all good gifts! Satan perverts them.

Avoid Pornography—It Is One of Satan's Alternatives to Marriage

A flawed battle plan won't encourage you to be honest. If you engage in pornography, acknowledge what God says about what you are doing. You do so to enjoy illicit sex. If that is true (and according to Jesus it is), you have only a few options that will please God. First, you have to stop sinning. I won't belabor that point here. It will be thoroughly covered throughout this book. But it doesn't matter one bit that all day long there are women who want to expose themselves to you on the Internet, on the job, at your school, or virtually wherever you may be. You must rely on the grace that God gives you to resist the temptation.

Second, you have to fix your marriage bed. In other words, you have to learn to lead your marriage in such a way that you experience the full blessing of oneness with your wife.[6] As the spiritual leader, you must take the steps to make sure that happens. Arrange for you and your spouse to get marital counseling. Find a good Christian marriage conference. As a couple, work through good books on Christian marriage that will provide you with healthy ways to address problem areas. But whatever you do, stop turning to Satan's pornographic ways to spice up or even replace intimacy with your wife.

Third, if you are single and struggling with sexual immorality of any kind, let me suggest one simple solution. I trust that you will gain many more throughout this book. Get a marriage bed. Discipline yourself for godliness and prepare yourself to be a spiritual leader and a provider. Then go out and find a godly Christian wife (Proverbs 18:22; 1 Corinthians 7:1–3, 8–9).[7]

RENEW YOUR MIND TO CONTROL YOUR EYES

Brothers, I fully realize how hard it is to do what I am charging you to do. I know all too well that the statistical scoreboard says that the church is losing ground in our war against pornography. But I also know that God is on our side; I know we can't just pack up and quit. So how do brothers hooked on porn win their secret sex wars? Again, you have to follow a biblical battle plan. If you let the mercies of God flood your heart with a love for God and you fill your mind with the Word of God, then the Spirit of God will renew and purify your mind (Romans 12:1-2). So renew your mind with the portions of Scripture that extol women as persons who bear the image of God. When you view women that way, God will arm you to fight like a spiritual warrior against pornography with the use of your mind and your eyes.

Focus on Her Person and Not Her Body Parts

Someone well said that a bird can land on your head, but you have to allow it to build a nest. It's not a sin to be tempted. It is a sin, however, to yield to it. The difference between brothers who win their battles for purity and those who lose them can be evidenced by what they do with their eyes. Be like Job and discipline your eyes to look women in the face and not everywhere else. Job wisely vowed, "I have made a covenant with my eyes; how then could I gaze at a virgin?" (Job 31:1). The verb for *gaze* is intensive. It refers to one's thoughts.

The secret to success is that if you don't look, you won't be able to visualize later. That is the insidious part of the lie "You can look but not touch." Once you look, your mind takes a digital picture, and it can then pop up in your brain at any time. That's why the act of looking doesn't just stop at looking. It always moves to thinking, and then to lusting, and then to sexual involvement. So don't be deceived. If she is immodest, then look away, turn the channel, close the computer window, and fight to not look back. In other words, take your head off of the swivel, and turn off your

X-ray vision. Practice letting your eyes be governed by biblical convictions and not by what women choose to wear or not wear.

It takes time to develop new habits, and it can be somewhat difficult. However, Christians can learn new habits by yielding to the Spirit of God for help. I plead with you to accept God's charge to guard your eyes before circumstances beyond your control lead you to make a decision in the heat of a moment. Be like Job. Set up your defensive battle line at the point of choosing to look or not look.

Never Give Up

Beware. The wink of an immoral woman is like the venom of a black widow. Solomon again warns, "For *many* are the victims she has cast down, and *numerous* are all her slain" (Proverbs 7:26). Perhaps right now you are hearing a whisper saying that it is too late. You've been bitten. You have looked and looked and now you can't stop looking. Brothers, that too is a lie from the pit of hell. You can stop, and there are many brothers who have and who no longer live in bondage to that devious master. But you must repent, by God's power.

Jesus charged us, "If your right eye makes you stumble, tear it out and throw it from you; for it is better for you to lose one of the parts of your body, than for your whole body to be thrown into hell" (Matthew 5:29). You must know that whatever Jesus commands us to do, He gives us abundant grace to do it. Here again, I plead with you to learn from David's flawed battle plan. Sadly, he chose to give in to his aroused carnal desires, so he kept looking at a nude woman who wasn't his wife, and that foolhardy decision changed his life, his family's lives, and the life of a nation.

PRIDE WILL LEAD TO MORAL FAILURE

There is a progression in the process of committing sexual sins. R. Kent Hughes, in *Disciplines of a Godly Man*, documents the chronology of moral falls as follows:

- The *desensitization* which happens through the conventional sensualities of culture.
- The deadly syndrome which comes through moral *relaxation* of discipline.
- The blinding effects of sensual *fixation*.
- And the *rationalization* of those in the grip of lust.

He concludes by explaining why God includes David's sinful pathology in His Holy Word: "Not only [is it] to instruct us, but to frighten us—to scare the sensuality right out of us!"[8]

No one just suddenly falls. You first have to let down your guard, then you have to tell yourself it's okay to do what God's Word says is evil. This is the perilous nature of our pride, and no one is immune from struggling with this sin. Proverbs 16:18 warns us that pride always comes before a fall.

In 2 Samuel 11:3, David inquired about the woman he saw to one of his servants. Veiled though his response was, David's servant placed his life in his hands and gave the king cautionary information about Bathsheba. He told David that she was married, implying that to sleep with her would be a capital offense. The law commanded that "if there is a man who commits adultery with another man's wife, one who commits adultery with his friend's wife, the adulterer and the adulteress shall surely be put to death" (Leviticus 20:10).

The servant brought to David's attention the fact that

the woman was the daughter of Eliam, and Eliam was one of David's highly esteemed mighty men (2 Samuel 11:3). It just so happened that Eliam's father was Ahithophel, who was David's chief counselor (2 Samuel 15:12). Bathsheba, then, was the granddaughter of David's personal counselor. If that were not sufficient to arrest his lust for her, the servant told David that her husband was Uriah, who was also one of David's valiant mighty men (2 Samuel 23:39). In so many words, David's humble servant bravely tried to lead the king to refrain from doing what he was lusting to do.

But David didn't stop, did he? This is the danger of flirting with sin. Once you start, it's hard to stop. Brothers, to be forewarned is to be forearmed. If you choose to use your leisure time in undisciplined ways, do not be surprised that you will see what you shouldn't look at. Moreover, you won't stop lusting after you look. Obey the tenth commandment and do not covet another man's wife. You won't go to bed with her if you don't lust after her. You won't yearn for her if you don't lustfully look at her. And you won't look at her with lust if you keep your mind's eye on the things that please God. Be humble and wise, heed the command not to look, and refrain from all leisure activities that lead you to lust.

LUST WILL LEAD TO MORAL FAILURE

In His grace, God had made David king of Israel, the most powerful man in the land. In turn, David used his God-given power to send his servant literally "to capture" Bathsheba. Brothers, God made us the stronger gender. It angers Him when we use that strength to plunder our sisters rather than to protect them. The Bible declares that this is what King David did. It states that after he commanded his messengers to take her, "he lay with her" (2 Samuel 11:4). David is clearly identified as the aggressor whose actions were driven by lust. In the end, everything that needs to be known is that David lusted for her, he took her, and he committed adultery. God condemned David's abuse of power through the prophet Nathan. He described David's sin, lamenting, "Why have you despised the word of the Lord by doing evil in His sight?" (2 Samuel 12:9a).

David became a prowler. Brothers, if looking at a naked woman did that to "a man after God's own heart," why do you think it will do anything less to you? Stop deceiving yourself. If you are fueling your carnal passions with any form of pornography, then you are turning yourself into a dangerous monster to every sister you know, and even to those in the church. Don't go down that road. The Bible plainly predicts that in the last days the church will be filled with so-called Christian brothers who love pleasure and love to prey on sisters (2 Timothy 3:1–8). All of us, therefore, need to guard our hearts and the church against predators.

David took Bathsheba, knowing that the punishment for adultery was death. Adultery is an odious, reprehensible sin. Proverbs 6:32 says, "The one who commits adultery with a woman is lacking sense; he who would destroy himself does it." Proverbs 6:33 adds, "Wounds and disgrace he will find, and his reproach will not be blotted out." If the consequences of adultery are so devastating, how and why do we do it? David's fall illustrates the answers to both of these questions very well.

Let me first explain how we commit the sin of adultery. Like David, we underestimate the deceiving and ensnaring power of our lust. The apostle James explains the path into sin like this, "Each one is tempted when he is carried away and enticed by his own lust" (James 1:14). James is saying that when we sin, we have no one to blame but ourselves. We sin because we yield to our own lust.

James puts it in the simple terms of fishing and hunting. He says that just like the bait on a fishing hook entices a fish to ignore the consequences of the hook and bite, so our lust entices us to bite into sin, ignoring its devastating consequences. Just as an animal goes for the bait and is netted and then dragged away by a hunter, so too your own lust entices you to go after the bait, allowing it to net and pull you into sin. Your lust blinds you to the dangers of sin and seduces you to believe that the sinful object of your desire is well worth the risk of getting hooked and trapped.

Practically, how does this lead a brother into the sin of adultery? It starts when you passively yield to your own lust and enjoy the desires of thinking romantically about someone other than your spouse. Once you bite that hook, your lust drags you deeper into the relationship by deceiving you into believing that it's okay to spend more time with her. Then it snares you by telling you that you can't deny your feelings. All the while, your lust never warns you that fanning your passions for someone other than your spouse is a perversion before God. Such passions are not true love.

Your lust then tells you that sinning in this way is worth it because you will get real appreciation, real love in return. So you give in and bite the forbidden fruit. You yield to your lust and commit adultery. The problem is that your lust has deceived you. It never told you the rest of what God says in James 1:15; that is, once sin is conceived, it carries with it the guaranteed payment of death.[9] When the sin is adultery, as in this case, it can result in the death of two marriages, not just one. It has the potential to destroy future marriages because it will affect your children, and perhaps even their children. It can ruin ministries. And worse, it causes spiritual separation from God. Take a moment and think of all the people who would become injured if you committed the sin of adultery.

The second question has been partly answered in the first. Why do we commit such a sin when we know God says that it is wrong and that it will lead to death? David explained why he committed this sin in Psalm 51:5. He said, "Behold, I was brought forth in iniquity, and in sin my mother conceived me." He's not blaming his mother. He is simply saying that he came to the shocking conclusion that from the moment he was born the capacity to commit this type of evil resided in him. Jesus would say the same. Adultery and fornication don't occur because of environmental circumstances. Sin is caused by the perversion of one's heart (Mark 7:20–23). Since that is our problem, reformation won't help. We need transformation from the inside out. God, and God alone, does that.

Brothers, we have to learn from the failure of the fallen warrior King David. When he was in the greatest battle of his life, he became passive. Instead of falling prey to this trap, brothers, let's aggressively fight according to the Word of God. Let's stand in true masculinity by applying the power of the Holy Spirit to subdue sin in our lives (Genesis 1:28).

A REFUSAL TO CONFESS AND REPENT WILL LEAD TO GREATER MORAL FAILURE

Finally, brothers, there is one last sobering warning we must draw from the fall of King David. It is this: if you choose not to heed the warning to stop living in sexual immorality, then your next sin may be greater than your last. David clearly sinned. Adultery is a horrible sin and results in horrible consequences. But if you are living the life of an unrepentant adulterer, your situation is not hopeless. Your best and only hope is to cast yourself on the mercy of God by confessing and repenting of your sin. Jesus forgives. And not only does He forgive, He also cleanses. And not only does He cleanse, He also makes new.

The good news is that Jesus is a heart surgeon. He never disappoints a patient who confesses his need for a clean heart (Psalm 51:10) and who, in faith, lies on His operating table. However, there is a catch. Jesus won't operate in the dark (1 John 1:5). You have to bring your secret sex struggles out from the dark and into the light. You must do that by confessing your sins to everyone you have sinned against as we are encouraged to do in James 5:16.

Brothers, that's hard, but that's the point, isn't it? Decisions made in the midst of war are always hard. But consider your alternative. It will be infinitely worse to continue to live as a slave to sexual sins, in which case, James assures you that doing so will result in spiritual death. I plead with you to trust God and confess your secret sins. But David didn't do that, did he? He refused to confess his sin. That fact gives us one more sobering lesson to avoid in our battles for purity.

Because David persisted in keeping his secret sex war in the darkness, he had to pay for his sin with a heavy price. Instead of confessing his sin before God, Bathsheba, and her husband, Uriah, he tried to cover his sin. First, he deceitfully called Uriah back from the war under the false pretense of getting an update on the battle. He did that hoping that Uriah would have sex with his wife. David wanted it to appear as though Uriah had impregnated her. Yet Uriah refused to enjoy his wife while his comrades were embroiled in a holy war. David repaid his officer's valor with more cowardice.

That's essentially what we do, brothers, when we yield to fear and don't confess our sins. David stooped as low as a brother can stoop. He decided to cover his sin with the blood of Uriah. David sent him back to the war, to the fiercest part of the battle, then he ordered the soldiers to abandon him so that he would be killed by the hand of his enemy. If you don't repent, then be warned. There is no limit to how low you can go. God hated what David did. According to 2 Samuel 11:27, "The thing that David had done was evil in the sight of the Lord." He added sin upon sin, and when he finally did repent, God added discipline upon discipline. Will you trust that God will forgive you? Brothers, I plead with you as someone who is a living witness of the redeeming grace of God, to repent and turn wholeheartedly to God with the confident hope that He will not cast you away.

CONCLUSION

None of this had to happen. David didn't have to look. David didn't have to lust. David didn't have to lie with another man's wife. David didn't have to try to conceal his sin, but he did. And because he made all of those choices, David lost the most important battle of his life.

I am glad that this is not the end of his story. Although David lost that battle, according to 1 Kings 15:5, he eventually won his personal war. He repented from his sin and made wiser choices. Let me encourage you that you too can win your war for sexual purity.

The best way to learn from David's foolish and wicked choices is to avoid making them yourself. Start engaging the battle for purity by resolving to win the battle with your eyes. You can live by the Spirit and exercise self-control over what you choose to look at. Next, turn to Christ and stop passively yielding to the temptation of your lust. God can fill you with His Spirit so that you long for Him more than for the carnal pleasure of illicit sex. You can do all of this and live a victorious life over sexual sin because the Bible says you can, and if God says that you can, He will give you the abundant grace to do it. Join the army of brothers who are living for the glory of God, for the love of Christ's church, for the honor of our sisters, and for a legacy of sexual purity to pass to our children.

Finally, if you have fallen, if you are a POW to sexual sin, let me encourage you that no matter how far you have fallen, it's not too late to repent. You don't have to live in defeat to sexual sins. That's the encouraging part of David's story—as dark as his sin was and as gripping as was his bondage to sexual sin, God delivered him. David reclaimed a life of purity.

In the epilogue, I will walk you through the steps David took and show you how you too can reclaim a life of purity.

 **POINTS OF REFLECTION**

1. When you choose sources of entertainment do you factor in how spiritually dangerous they can be?

   ♦ Read Ephesians 5:1–13 and Philippians 4:8–9. Use these passages to write out standards to govern the types of entertainment you will and won't use in your leisure time.
   ♦ What do you think would be different about the way a man thought about women who for years looked at anything that appeared on cable TV versus a man who for years filled his mind only with things that were consistent with Ephesians 5:1–13 and Philippians 4:8?

2. Have you ever made a covenant with your eyes as to how you will and won't look at a woman who is not your wife?

   ♦ Read Philippians 4:11–13. Have you learned the secret of being content in knowing that if you have Christ you have enough; and therefore, you don't need pornography or more sex? We need more of Christ and more of the knowledge of what we have in Him.
   ♦ Which biblical battle plan principles do you need to start applying in order to avoid the temptation of lusting for pornography? For example, do you need to stop dragging your feet and get married (1 Corinthians 7:8–9)?
   ♦ Do you really believe Jesus when He said that sins of lust endanger one's soul with going to hell (Matthew 5:28–30)? Are you willing to get radical in your repentance in order to cut off any enslaving sexual habits?

3. Do you heed caution when you hear a sermon, or when a friend challenges you to avoid sexually tempting situations? In other words, do you listen to the people whom God has in your life who would speak to you in the way that Nathan spoke to David?

4. Are you moving toward a moral fall with a particular woman? Or are you presently involved in an adulterous relationship or fornicating with someone? What does James 1:13–16 say about how you got into that situation?

5. Are you prepared to confess your secret sins and repent from them? Consider taking the following steps.

   ◆ Meditate on Psalm 32 and Psalm 51.
   ◆ What happened to David because he chose not to confess? Read 2 Samuel 11:5–13. What changed when he did?
   ◆ Read Psalm 10:4, 10–11, 13. According to these verses, what are you saying about God if you choose not to repent?
   ◆ Confess your sin to God and to whomever else you have sinned against.

LIVING FREE FROM THE SLAVERY OF SEXUAL SIN

A Battle Plan that Will Set You Free
Romans 6:19–23

— **Pastor Victor G. Sholar**

BROTHERS, there is a well-known saying that issues a profound warning: If we do not learn from the problems of the past, we are bound to repeat them in the future. Thus, I want to share with you an interesting fact from American history that parallels the problems we are facing today.

The time was 1787; the place was Philadelphia; and the event was the drafting of the United States Constitution. When the framers of this most significant document faced the dilemma of determing each state's level of representation, they concluded that three-fifths of the slave population should be counted. In doing so, they concluded that slaves were less than human, only three-fifths human.

As African Americans, we faced this hideous problem

over two hundred years ago. Moreover, it has a cruel irony to it. Eleven years earlier on July 4, 1776, at the same place, Philadelphia, fifty-six representatives of the thirteen colonies signed the Declaration of Independence. The second sentence of this historic document, which was drafted by Thomas Jefferson, read: "We hold these truths to be self-evident, that all men are created equal, that they are endowed by their Creator with certain unalienable rights; that among these are Life, Liberty, and the pursuit of Happiness."

It is interesting that the founding fathers acknowledged the self-evident truth that *all men are created equal*, and at the same time some of those same men eleven years later would regard African American residents of this new nation as less than human. As a result of this noticeable disparity, slaves were denied the opportunity to exercise their God-given, unalienable rights, which included *life, liberty, and the pursuit of happiness.*

This sad fact in American history has a corresponding spiritual truth that speaks clearly to the problems we are facing today. In Genesis 1:27–31, Scripture says that God created man in His own image. Then He endowed man with an innate desire for life, liberty, and the pursuit of true happiness in Him. Unfortunately, due to man's fall into sin, man has consequently become enslaved to lust and lawlessness, which then leads to hell (Ecclesiastes 7:29; John 3:19–20; Revelation 21:8).

As a result of man's enslavement to sin, he has become less than human in a moral sense.[1] Ecclesiastes 7:29 attests to this truth. Even though man still retains the image of God in his person (Genesis 9:6; James 3:9), his nature has been marred, or damaged, by sin. The apostle Paul put it like this in Romans 3:12: "All [of mankind] have turned aside, together they have become useless [unprofitable or worthless]." Sin has so corrupted, distorted, and twisted man's nature that God regards all of unregenerate mankind as useless, worthless, or unprofitable.

You might ask, "What does this have to do with me and the subject of sexual sin?" That is a good question because the problems we face in the war against sexual sin have everything to do with the issue of slavery. According to *Webster's Dictionary and Thesaurus*, one definition of the word *slave* is: "one who has lost all powers of resistance to some pernicious habit or vice."[2] The word *pernicious* means "having the quality of causing destruction or injury."

Now, I must be honest with you. The problem we are facing today in our churches and communities is that the pernicious habit of sexual sin is enslaving many African Americans. This slavery may not be on the same level as the racist slavery that existed 220 years ago, but it is equally as degrading, humiliating, destructive, and overpowering. The enslavement to sexual sin has not only caused its victims to function as less than human from a moral perspective, it is also threatening genocide for the entire African American community. Consider the following statistics:

In the United States, the HIV/AIDS epidemic is a health crisis for African Americans. At all stages of HIV/AIDS—from infection with HIV to death with AIDS—blacks (including African Americans) are disproportionately affected compared with members of other races and ethnicities.

HIV/AIDS in 2005

◆ According to the 2000 census, blacks make up approximately 13% of the U.S. population. However, in 2005, blacks accounted for 18,121 (49%) of the estimated 37,331

111

new HIV/AIDS diagnoses in the United States in the thirty-three states with long-term, confidential, name-based HIV reporting.

◆ Of all black men living with HIV/AIDS, the *primary* transmission category was sexual contact with other men, followed by injection drug use and high-risk heterosexual contact.

◆ Of all black women living with HIV/AIDS, the *primary* transmission category was high-risk heterosexual contact, followed by injection drug use.

◆ Of the estimated 141 infants prenatally infected with HIV, 91 (65%) were black (CDC, HIV/AIDS Reporting System, unpublished data, December 2006). Of the estimated 18,849 people under the age of twenty-five whose diagnosis of HIV/AIDS was made during 2001–2004 in the thirty-three states with HIV reporting, 11,554 (61%) were black.

AIDS in 2005

◆ Blacks accounted for 20,187 (50%) of the estimated 40,608 AIDS cases diagnosed in the fifty states and the District of Columbia.

◆ The rate of AIDS diagnoses for black adults and adolescents was ten times the rate for whites and nearly three times the rate for Hispanics. The rate of AIDS diagnoses for black women was nearly twenty-three times the rate for white women. The rate of AIDS diagnoses for black men was eight times the rate for white men.

◆ The 185,988 blacks living with AIDS in the fifty states and the District of Columbia accounted for 44% of the 421,873 people in those areas living with AIDS.

◆ Of the sixty-eight U.S. children (younger than thirteen years of age) who had a new AIDS diagnosis, forty-six were black.

◆ Since the beginning of the epidemic, blacks have accounted for 397,548 (42%) of the estimated 952,629 AIDS cases diagnosed in the fifty states and the District of Columbia.

◆ From the beginning of the epidemic through December 2005, an estimated 211,559 blacks with AIDS died.

◆ Of persons whose diagnosis of AIDS had been made during 1997–2004, a smaller proportion of blacks (66%) were alive after nine years compared with American Indians and Alaska Natives (67%), Hispanics (74%), whites (75%), and Asians and Pacific Islanders (81%).

Sexual Risk Factors

Black women are most likely to be infected with HIV as a result of sex with men who are infected with HIV. They may not be aware of their male partners' possible risk factors for HIV infection, such as unprotected sex with multiple partners, bisexuality, or injection drug use. Sexual contact is also the main risk factor for black men. Male-to-male sexual contact was the *primary* risk factor for 48% of black men with HIV/AIDS at the end of 2005, and

high-risk heterosexual contact was the *primary* risk factor
for 22% *(emphases added)*.

The highest rates of sexually transmitted diseases (STDs) are
those for blacks. In 2005, blacks were about eighteen times
as likely as whites to have gonorrhea and about five times as
likely to have syphilis. Partly because of physical changes
caused by STDs, including genital lesions that can serve as
an entry point for HIV, the presence of certain STDs can increase one's chances of contracting HIV infection three- to
five-fold. Similarly, a person who has both HIV infection and
certain STDs has a greater chance of spreading HIV to others.

A recent CDC literature review showed that high rates of
HIV infection for black MSM *(men having sex with men)*
may be partly attributable to a high prevalence of STDs
that facilitate HIV transmission[3] *(emphases added)*.

Brothers, considering these facts, think about how likely
our people would be to want to continue in sexual sin,
knowing the high risk of contracting a deadly disease such
as HIV/AIDS. Yet oddly, our society would conclude that
this epidemic is an educational problem (not enough facts
disseminated to warn people of the dangers of these diseases
and how they are transmitted). Society would also claim
that it is an economic problem (not enough funds allocated
for programs to train people on how to protect themselves).
Furthermore, society might even place the blame on an environmental problem (the poverty-stricken areas of our
country are where the highest percentages of sexually transmitted diseases occur).

But the fact of the matter is that it is not an educational
problem (everyone is aware of how these diseases are trans-

mitted, or else we wouldn't call them "sexually transmitted diseases" [STDs]); nor is it an economic problem (millions of dollars are being spent on prevention programs yet millions of people are still contracting STDs); nor is it an environmental problem (poverty-stricken areas are not the only places where people contract STDs).

The real problem is spiritual enslavement to sin. There is no other way to explain how people who have been created in the image of God, with intelligence and an ability to know right from wrong, can continue on the path of self-destruction through engaging in sexual sin. Consider a very important passage of Scripture that addresses this epidemic of slavery to sin. Though this passage doesn't directly speak of sexual sin, it is relevant for us in discerning the powerful mastery of sin overall. Only God, through the Gospel and the power of His Spirit, can deliver us from sin's enslavement and grant us true life, liberty, and the pursuit of happiness.

Before I proceed, I want to make a case that sin, in whatever form you may be involved, does not bring satisfaction as much as living a holy life. It's important that you understand this because many of us are foolishly self-confident when it comes to avoiding the repercussions for sexual sin. That's why I'm not convinced that statistics alone about the dangers of contracting a sexually transmitted disease are going to stop anyone from having sex. After all, we are shrewd enough to use a contraceptive, masturbate, or have oral sex in hopes of avoiding the consequences.

In fact, the Centers for Disease Control estimated in 2002 that young people between the ages of thirteen and twenty-five are contracting HIV at a rate of two every hour. Yet, in the same year, the federal government allocated at least $427.7 million for teen sex education and contraception programs in hopes of teaching young people how to avoid contracting sexually transmitted diseases.[4] Therefore, my objective is to convince you that any type of sexual sin is enslaving, degrading, and destructive; but purity of life is satisfying and fulfilling.

In Romans 6:19–23, the apostle Paul contrasts the shameful results of being under sin's mastery with the sanctifying blessings of being enslaved to God. So I want to give you two advantages of being enslaved to God: (1) The work is not shameful and the pay isn't death (6:19–21); and (2) The benefits are sanctifying and the gift is eternal life (6:22–23).

1. THE WORK IS NOT SHAMEFUL AND THE PAY ISN'T DEATH

In Romans 6:19–21, the apostle Paul stated:

I am speaking in human terms because of the weakness of your flesh. For just as you presented your members as slaves to impurity and to lawlessness, resulting in further lawlessness, so now present your members as slaves to righteousness, resulting in sanctification. For when you were slaves of sin, you were free in regard to righteousness. Therefore what benefit were you then deriving from the things of which you are now ashamed? For the outcome of those things is death.

When Paul wrote, "I am speaking in human terms because of the weakness of your flesh," he was simply saying, "I am using the analogy of slavery to help you understand the spiritual truth about the control that sin or righteousness has over the person who submits himself to one of the two (paraphrase mine)." In the previous verses (15–18), Paul had corrected the false notion that a person can claim to be a Christian and still live a sinful lifestyle. His point was that the person who places his life near either sin or righteousness is in reality demonstrating who his master is. In other words, if you gravitate toward sin all the time, with no genuine repentance, then you are a slave of sin. On the other hand, if you gravitate toward righteousness all the time, out of a love for the Lord Jesus Christ, then you are a slave of righteousness.

Brothers, the question I pose to you right now is: what do you enjoy more, sin or righteousness? Whatever you find the most pleasure in identifies your master. Your pleasures are either enslaved to sin or enslaved to righteousness. But in Romans 6:17–18, Paul explained to the Roman believers that though they used to live a life of sin, they became obedient "from the heart to that form of teaching [the gospel]" to which they were committed, and as a result they were immediately freed from the power of sin and became slaves of righteousness (my paraphrase).

Have you experienced this truth as a result of turning from your sins and trusting in the Lord Jesus Christ as Romans 10:9–10 presents the way to achieve salvation? If you have, then the Gospel promises to change your heart from having a love for sin to having a love for righteousness (2 Corinthians 5:17; 1 Peter 2:24). Now, this doesn't mean you will never sin again in this life, but the Gospel will change your heart so that you will no longer have a desire to be enslaved to sin's power (Romans 7:14–25).

The reason Paul selected slavery as an illustration for the power that either sin or righteousness has over a person's life is because slavery was common to the believers in the Roman Empire. Of the one hundred twenty million people in the empire, one half were slaves, and many of those were Christians. However, speaking in "human terms" or in an analogy about slavery may seem inadequate to some degree since the analogy doesn't fully explain the unique relationship every true Christian has with God. But it does help to drive home the point that the one you enjoy serving the most is the one who really is your master.

Paul further wrote, "For just as you presented your members as slaves to impurity and to lawlessness, resulting in further lawlessness" (Romans 6:19b). The word *for* is given here to remind us of the fact stated in verse 17, that "You were slaves of sin." In other words, when you were enslaved to sin, you lived a life constantly under the power of impurity and lawlessness. The word *impurity* means moral uncleanness, filth, and lewdness. It describes being spiritually nasty or morally offensive. The word we could use today to describe impurity would be *scandalous*. In Romans 1:24, Paul reminds us that when we were in a state of rebellion against God, He gave us over in the lusts of our hearts to impurity, that our bodies might be dishonored among us.

When we were slaves of sin, we dishonored our bodies, whether it was done through fornication (sexual intercourse and oral sex outside of marriage), adultery, homosexuality (living on the down-low), or any other form of sexual sin (masturbation). Sin was our master, or better stated, our pimp, and we loved it. Before salvation, we enjoyed being spiritually scandalous or morally filthy. The way in which we joked was filthy; what we desired to watch on television was filthy (pornography); the plans for how we spent our weekends were filthy. Our entire being (mind, will, and emotions) was shackled to spiritual nastiness. And the sad thing about it was that we had no shame!

The next word Paul used is *lawlessness*, which means rebellion against God and His law. It is a refusal to submit oneself to God's authority. We live as if God and His law do not exist. This aspect of sin clearly exposes the heart of the problem we are now facing, not only in the African American community, but in our nation as a whole when it comes to sexual sin. It also explains why we are reaping the consequences for our actions. In the endnotes read the excerpt titled, "Abstinence-Only-Until-Marriage Programs: Ineffective, Unethical, and Poor Public Health," and consider the lawless justification against abstinence being taught in schools.[5]

Brothers, we do not have any human rights that run counter to God's Word. To claim that we have the right to choose the type of lifestyle we want is to commit the sin of lawlessness. Abortion, homosexuality, adultery, and fornication (sex outside of marriage) are not issues of politics, opinion polls, or religion. Rather, they are serious offenses against a holy God who has created us to love and serve Him alone. That is why we are suffering the harmful consequences of lawlessness, including emotional and social problems caused by sexually transmitted diseases.

Consider these questions: How is it that a man and a woman can be celibate or abstinent before marriage, get married and enjoy sexual intimacy within the covenant of marriage for many years, and not contract a single sexually transmitted disease? How can they be 100 percent free from the fear of contracting an STD (though they have been intimate numerous times) as opposed to those who contract an STD due to sexual promiscuity?

How can sexually transmitted diseases be regulated in this way? In Hebrews 13:4 we get the answer: "Marriage is to be held in honor among all [regardless of political persuasion, religious background, or personal preference], and the marriage bed is to be undefiled; for fornicators and adulterers God will judge." Note that in 1 Corinthians 6:9–10 the Bible also includes homosexuals in this category.

The writer of the book of Hebrews regards sexual intimacy between a married couple (male and female) as undefiled or without moral pollution. But notice the warning that the author gives to those who don't honor the marriage covenant: "For fornicators and adulterers God will judge." This is a promise by a God who cannot lie to those who disrespect His commandments. He will judge the sexually immoral. There are temporal judgments that God will bring in this life, which may come in different ways or forms; nonetheless, they are the consequences of lawless rebellion. Such are the results of this dire state:

> Emotional, social and cognitive development continues well past adolescence. With their still developing brains, teens do not yet possess the ability to either fathom the physical and emotional consequences of sex or to deal with them once they happen. The "early initiation into sexual behaviors is taking a toll on teens' mental health" with dependency on boyfriends and girlfriends, serious depression around breakups and cheating, and suffering from a lack of goals as possible results. As "teenagers are not mature enough to know all the ramifications of what they're doing," "early sexual activity—whether in or out of a romantic relationship—does far more harm than good."[6]

Although these are stated to be harmful emotional and social consequences for sexual sin among our teens, we as adults are not immune to such consequences ourselves. There is an eternal judgment that God will bring upon fornicators, adulterers, homosexuals, and those who commit murder through abortion. Moreover, by considering this judgment, I believe it is correct to say that there is no such thing as "safe sex" outside the bonds of marriage. Therefore,

Paul commands believers to "present your members as slaves to righteousness, resulting in sanctification" (Romans 6:19).

The fact that Paul could issue the command to present yourself as a slave of righteousness affirms the truth he stated in the previous verse, "having been freed from sin, you became slaves of righteousness" (v. 18). God has already freed you from sin's degrading and destructive power. Now, you are a slave of righteousness. As a believer, the Bible says in 2 Peter 1:3 that you have "everything pertaining to life and godliness." All you have to do is live it out. Now, the question becomes, how? In Romans 6:19, Paul continued to answer, "For *just as* you presented your members as slaves to impurity and lawlessness . . . *so now* present your members as slaves to righteousness."

Did you notice the two phrases highlighted in italics, "just as" and "so now"? Paul was simply saying, "In the same way you used to serve sin, now serve righteousness." You see, living a life of righteousness only changes who you serve, not how you serve. In other words, as slaves under the power of impurity and lawlessness, we joyfully rendered our minds, hearts, and lives in obedience to them. Now, we are to take those same members and joyfully render them as servants of righteousness. You were good at sin because you loved it. Now become good at righteousness by loving it, and the result will be that you will grow in sanctification, which is holiness.

In Romans 6:20, Paul stated, "For when you were slaves of sin, you were free in regard to righteousness." This verse explains why you should present yourselves as slaves of righteousness. When you were under the degrading mastery of sin, you were not under the blessings of being a slave to righteousness. Paul asserted that you should be motivated to present your life to righteousness because of the dark life you lived under your former master; that is, sin.

Do you remember how you used to be? Have you forgotten why you wanted freedom from sin? Do you remember when you were broken and shamed by the evils you committed? Do you remember when you became tired of the guilt? Do you remember how you tried to reform your life by doing good on your own, apart from Jesus Christ, and how that did not bring the peace of conscience you were longing for? Do you remember the day you cried out to God in prayer to deliver you from your sins? Do you remember that? Sometimes we need to dig up the terrible memories of our past life so we can appreciate our present situation. Listen, sin hasn't changed. If it didn't benefit you then, what makes you think it will benefit you now?

That is exactly Paul's conclusion for why we should present ourselves as slaves to righteousness: "Therefore what benefit were you then deriving from the things of which you are now ashamed? For the outcome of those things is death" (Romans 6:21).

The word *benefit* means profit or advantage. And the question is: what benefit, profit, or advantage did you gain when you lived a life of impurity and lawlessness? Or let me put it like this: How did living a life of impurity benefit your thought life after salvation? How did sexual immorality prepare you for marriage? What advantage did sexual promiscuity have in helping you learn how to have a meaningful nonsexual relationship with others? How did masturbation help you to satisfy your wife? If you are single, what profit will masturbation, oral sex, or fornication have in teaching you how to love your future wife as Christ loves the church as commanded in Ephesians 5:25? How will any sexual sin glorify God? First Corinthians 6:18–20 reveals why this is not even possible.

It is surprising to see some Christians believing that sin can bring more benefit in ministering to others than the effect that righteous living would bring. There is a certain mind-set in the church today that if you commit an act of sin it somehow qualifies you to be effective in ministering to others who have committed a similar sin. This is a lie! Committing sin doesn't help anyone to be more effective in counseling sinners; in fact, it has the potential to have the opposite effect. If someone is misled by following a wrong example, they may become more convinced not to fight against their enslaving sin and instead become comfortable with it. Galatians 6:1 offers the qualifications for ministering to those who are caught in a sin. That person must be spiritually mature and possess the qualities of humility and gentleness.

Living a life of impurity and lawlessness doesn't profit or benefit anyone. Conversely, Paul warned in Romans 6:21 that such a life brings shame: "The things of which you are now ashamed." He finished this verse by saying that "the outcome of those things [impurity and lawlessness] is death." Living a life of sin was not only shameful, degrading, humiliating, scandalous, and unprofitable, but as sinners, we were headed to eternal separation from God in hell.

2. THE BENEFITS ARE SANCTIFYING AND THE GIFT IS ETERNAL LIFE

Paul stated in Romans 6:22–23:

But now having been freed from sin and enslaved to God, you derive your benefit, resulting in sanctification, and the outcome, eternal life. For the wages of sin is death, but the free gift of God is eternal life in Christ Jesus our Lord.

When Paul wrote, "Having been freed from sin and enslaved to God" (v. 22), he was speaking of what God has done for us by His grace and not what we have done on our own. When we were sinners, we had no power to free ourselves from sin's mastery and make ourselves slaves to God. In John 8:34–36, Jesus tells us that only He can free us from sin. It is the work of God's sanctifying grace alone that gives us the power to choose God as our Master. The benefit, profit, or advantage we received from being freed from sin and enslaved to God is sanctification (moral cleanness, purity). Romans 6:4 reveals that this brings the newness or freshness of life that comes through freedom from sin.

Therefore, living a life of purity is what it means to be truly human. Holiness recovers what man lost in sin—moral dignity and nobility. Therefore, he is no longer morally less than human, but rather he is becoming more and more human. You see, we have not reached our purpose for being human until we are sanctified. Sanctification is the process by which fallen man becomes whole again, in regard to holiness.

I am afraid that we have become so conditioned by sin that somehow we think being a human is synonymous with being a sinner. We have been programmed to believe that for us to be "real" we must be open about our sinfulness, as if that makes us manly. You have heard the saying, "To err is human." But to err is not human; it's subhuman, abnormal. Yet the world says exactly the opposite. It says to be holy is to be abnormal or subhuman. You may recall the advertisement of the movie called *The 40 Year Old Virgin*. It portrayed a forty-year-old man who was out of touch with the reality of today's culture. His style of clothing was outdated, which made him look really goofy and dorky. You see, the world mocks virginity as being abnormal or subhuman.

But the truth is that sanctification is reshaping or reconstructing what was marred by sin back into its original design: the image of God, or more specifically, the image of Christ (Romans 8:29; 2 Corinthians 3:18; Ephesians 4:23–24).

Paul continued, "And the outcome, eternal life" (Romans 6:22). Though the context here would suggest the quantity of life we will experience when we are in heaven, I believe it also addresses the quality of life we should experience right now. Now the question is: what does the quality of life mean? In John 17:3, Jesus didn't define eternal life as going to heaven or living forever, but as knowing God the Father, which means having a relationship with Him. This relationship with God begins at the moment we trust in Christ and continues in heaven. You see, man is not complete in his being until he knows God. Augustine said it best, "You have made us, O Lord, for Yourself, and our heart will find no rest until it rests in You."[7] This is what the quality of life means.

Now get this, sanctification is a privilege, because we don't deserve to be in a relationship with God. Sanctification and having a relationship with God are one and the same because sanctification is not possible if you don't desire God. We often divorce relationship, joy, and pleasure from holy living, but this is not what the Bible teaches. Our Lord Jesus Christ taught in Matthew 22:37–40 that the whole Old Testament rests upon loving the Lord God with all your heart, and with all your soul, and with all your mind.

The heart, soul, and mind involves our thoughts and affections. In other words, Jesus described obedience to the greatest commandment as setting one's thoughts and affections upon God in a loving relationship. I believe it is fair to say that if we fail to obey the greatest commandment by loving and enjoying God with all our heart, then we have committed the greatest sin; that is, we have abandoned our first love and must repent before God (see Revelation 2:4–5).

Therefore, sanctification will progress in your life as your enjoyment and delight in God increases, until the completion of your salvation in heaven when you will experience what David said in Psalm 16:11, "In Your presence is fullness of joy; in Your right hand there are pleasures forever." C. S. Lewis was correct when he wrote, "How little people know who think that holiness is dull. When one meets the real thing, it is irresistible."[8] So the believer truly has life, liberty, and the pursuit of happiness as a present possession—because he belongs to God.

Paul concluded this section by writing, "For the wages of sin is death, but the free gift of God is eternal life in Christ Jesus our Lord" (Romans 6:23). A person does not profit anything from being a slave of sin in the long run, because eventually that slavery leads to hell. Therefore, Paul's point is strengthened by the fact that we should present ourselves as slaves of righteousness resulting in sanctification. That is the benefit of receiving the free gift of God, which is eternal life in Christ Jesus, our Lord.

CONCLUSION

It was the great preacher Phillip Brooks who said, "No man in this world attains to freedom from any slavery except by entrance into some higher servitude. There is no such thing as an entirely free man conceivable."[9] Brothers, our Lord Jesus Christ has granted us freedom in salvation; we are slaves of righteousness. We have been given a much higher, nobler, and fulfilling life than the dehumanizing life of being a slave to sin.

But this truth will not be experienced in your life if you are being "conformed to this world," instead of being "transformed by the renewing of your mind, so that you may prove what the will of God is, that which is good and acceptable and perfect" (Romans 12:2). So I appeal to you, in the name of Christ, who gave His life to liberate you from a life of slavery to sexual sins—use your freedom to live as Christ's slaves of righteousness.

POINTS OF REFLECTION

1. In Romans 6:18, Paul wrote that every true Christian has been "freed from sin." Conversely, they have become "slaves of righteousness." As a professing Christian, how is this truth manifested in your life with regard to sexual purity? Are you living free from this enslaving sin? Is it fair to say that if your life is lived under the mastery of sexual sin that you may not be a Christian?

2. In Romans 6:19, Paul wrote, "For just as you presented your members as slaves to impurity and to lawlessness . . . so now present your members as slaves to righteousness." How are you presenting your mind, heart, and body to the impurity and lawlessness of sexual sin? In what ways can you now begin to present those same members "as slaves to righteousness?" (Read Romans 12:1–2; 13:13–14; Galatians 5:16–24; Philippians 4:8.)

3. In Romans 6:21, Paul wrote, "What benefit were you then deriving from the things of which you are now ashamed? For the outcome of those things is death." What are the ungodly influences in your life that are tempting you to believe that sexual sin will benefit your Christian walk? List these ungodly influences (for example, movies, magazines, friends, dating relationships, etc.). How does the Lord want you to deal with these ungodly influences? (Read Matthew 5:27–30; Ephesians 5:1–5; 1 Thessalonians 4:3–8; 5:22; 1 Peter 2:11; 4:1–5.)

4. In Romans 6:22, Paul wrote, "But now having been freed from sin and enslaved to God, you derive your benefit,

resulting in sanctification, and the outcome, eternal life." List ten benefits of abstaining from sexual sin. How many of these benefits are you applying to your life presently? What benefits are you not applying?

5. In the chapter, I stated that, "A life of purity is what it means to be truly human. Holiness recovers what man lost in sin—moral dignity and nobility. . . . Sanctification and re-lationship with God are one and the same because sanctifi-cation is not possible if you don't desire God. We often divorce relationship, joy, and pleasure from holy living, but this is not what the Bible teaches." If living a holy life corre-sponds to having joy in God, in what ways can you maintain your joy in God in the fight against sexual sin so that holi-ness can progress in your life? What must you do when sex-ual sin has disrupted your joy of relationship with God? (Read Psalm 32:1–7; 34:8–14; 51; 73; 103:1–5; 1 Peter 2:1–3.)

FREQUENTLY ASKED QUESTIONS

1. Doesn't sex before marriage help prepare you to be sexually compatible with your wife?

No, it does not! The Bible describes marriage as a covenant of companionship between a man and a woman (Genesis 2:18–25; Malachi 2:15–16). Sexual sin, even with the woman you are engaged to, will not prepare you for companionship in marriage. True love is self-sacrificing for the spiritual good of the other person. Ask yourself, "How can I love a woman when I am being a stumbling block to her by causing her to sin against God? How am I benefiting her walk with Christ?"

Sexual immorality never helps to develop your ability to

love in a Christlike way, because it is a sin that is fueled by self-centered desires. What do you think is going to happen when that woman is no longer "sexually compatible"? When the sex is not as great as it used to be? What are you going to do? Seek someone else to gratify your sinful longings? The way in which you answer these questions will reveal whether you have a Christ-centered love or self-centered lust.

Living a life of purity by learning how to love others sacrificially prepares you for a life of sacrificial love toward your wife. You will learn how not to seek your own interest but the interest of others (Philippians 2:1–5). You see, sacrificial love toward others is a sign of humility, while self-centered lust is a sign of pride. The reason self-centered lust is a sign of pride is because you think you are better than others, that's why you treat them any way you want. You don't care that the sexual act is harming the person you are with in a spiritual way, even though the act is consensual.

Also, practicing sexual immorality with the woman to whom you are engaged is a violation of the Tenth Commandment, "You shall not covet your neighbor's house [or household]" (from Exodus 20:17). Though the parents or guardians may approve of you marrying their daughter, that doesn't mean you have the right to violate her sexually before you are married. Therefore, you are committing sin not only against your fiancée but her parents as well. It is very important for you to understand this: it is only on the wedding day when the parents have officially handed over their daughter to you, and the vows have been made, when sex can be properly viewed as an expression of love and romance (Genesis 2:24–25; Deuteronomy 22:13–21; 1 Corinthians 7:36–38).

Therefore, demonstrating sacrificial love is the exact opposite of engaging in sexual immorality with a woman. It involves looking out for the spiritual welfare of others because you want God's will to be done in their lives (see 1 Thessalonians 4:3–8). This attitude is a sign of true humility.

2. Is masturbation a sin?

Yes! Masturbation, or self sex, is a form of sexual sin because it is a misuse of the sexual organ which God created to be used in the marriage relationship. Therefore, when you commit this sinful act you are involved in self-centered lust. Masturbation doesn't prepare you for marriage. It actually hinders your ability to satisfy your future spouse in sexual intimacy. It also poisons your thoughts because you must mentally think on sensual things in order to arouse yourself.

In summary, here is some practical wisdom Solomon gives on how to abstain from sexual sin:

Do not desire [lust after] her beauty in your heart (Proverbs 6:25). This truth applies to pornography. In other words, guard your thoughts from sensual images.

Keep your way far from her, and do not go near the door of her house (Proverbs 5:8). Physical distance is a sure safeguard from sexual sin. Don't be foolish enough to be alone with a woman—you are thereby asking to be tempted.

Drink water from your own cistern and fresh water from your own well. Should your springs be dispersed abroad, streams of water in the streets? Let them be yours alone and not for strangers with you. Let your fountain be blessed, and rejoice in the wife of your youth. As a loving hind and a graceful doe, let her breasts satisfy you at all times; be exhilarated always with her love (Proverbs

5:15–19). Enjoy sex with your own wife. If you are single, trust in Christ's unfailing strength to keep you pure and satisfied until He blesses you with marriage. (Read 1 Corinthians 7:32–35.)

PUTTING SIN TO DEATH

⬆ A Battle Plan to Win a War Unto Death
Colossians 3:5–7[1]

— Pastor H. B. Charles

HE was only twenty-one years old. This brave young man was in the midst of enjoying a spectacular career as one of Spain's most brilliant and celebrated matadors. He was handily winning the bullfight that fateful day in 1985. But Jose Cubero made a tragic mistake that proved to be fatal. After the initial takedown, Jose firmly thrust his sword a final time into a bleeding, delirious bull. To the crowd's delight, the wounded bull collapsed into the dirt.

Considering the struggle finished, Jose turned to the crowd to acknowledge the applause. The bull, however, was not dead; neither was it about to give up the fight. Without Cubero noticing, the dying bull rose to its feet and lunged at the unsuspecting matador one last time. Its horns pierced the young man's back and punctured his heart. Sadly, this premature celebration led to a permanent casualty.

Let this be a warning, brothers. It can happen to you! You—your family, your witness, and your ministry—can become a spiritual casualty if you do not fight sin to the death. Please do not fool yourself. None of us have reached perfection yet. You are not immune to temptation. Given the right tempting opportunity, any of us could fall into gross sin that betrays the ones we love, costs us our spiritual influence, and dishonors the name of the Lord. So I challenge you to take heed to the message of Colossians 3:5–7, "Put to death therefore what is earthly in you: sexual immorality, impurity, passion, evil desire, and covetousness, which is idolatry. On account of these the wrath of God is coming. In these you too once walked, when you were living in them."

We have three enemies of the soul: the world, the Devil, and the flesh. But the Lord Jesus Christ has defeated each of these enemies to the glory of God. This decisive defeat was accomplished through the birth, life, death, burial, resurrection, and ascension of the Lord Jesus. However, the final destruction of these enemies of the soul will not be consummated until the second coming of Christ. Do not miss that! Our spiritual enemy is doomed, but the Enemy continues to attack by stealth to undermine your faith in God and overthrow your fruitfulness for God.

Think about it. The Lord Jesus has overcome the world. God the Father has ordained a day when His kingdom will come and His will is going to be done on earth as it is in heaven. Every knee will bow to Christ and every tongue will confess that Jesus is Lord of all. Yet the sin-corrupted value system of this world is still opposed to God. This is why Paul says,

Do not be conformed to this world, but be transformed by the renewal of your mind, that by testing you may discern what is the will of God, what is good and acceptable and perfect. (Romans 12:2)

In addition, John says,

Do not love the world or the things in the world. If anyone loves the world, the love of the Father is not in him. For all that is in the world—the desires of the flesh and the desires of the eyes and pride in possessions—is not from the Father but is from the world. And the world is passing away along with its desires, but whoever does the will of God abides forever. (1 John 2:15–17)

Likewise, the Devil has been defeated. Read the end of the story. There is no Devil in the opening two chapters of the Bible. And there is no Devil in the final two chapters of the Bible. Hallelujah! The Lord Jesus has disarmed the evil rulers and authorities and put them to open shame by triumphing over them on the cross (Colossians 2:13–15). Yet the Devil is still prowling about like a roaring lion, seeking whom he may devour (1 Peter 5:8). We must continue to submit to God and resist the Devil so that he will flee from us (James 4:7).

This is also true of our sinful flesh. Jesus Christ has delivered the final deathblow to sin. But we must destroy the influence of sin in our lives day by day. Colossians 3:1–4 says, "If then you have been raised with Christ, seek the things that are above, where Christ is, seated at the right hand of God. Set your mind on things that are above, not on things that are on earth. For you have died, and your life is hidden with Christ in God. When Christ who is your life appears, then you also will appear with him in glory."

Then Colossians 3:5 issues a command: "Put to death therefore what is earthly in you." Do you feel the tension between these two statements? The old, sinful *you* died when you trusted Christ for salvation. But we still struggle against the will of God. The sin nature has been defeated but it has not totally changed. You died to sin. It has not died to you. Therefore, you must put to death what is earthly in you. Write it down. Every believer is engaged in an ongoing struggle against sin.

As you read this, you may be wondering: can I really be saved if I still struggle against sin? That's a good question. The answer is even better. Brothers, the fact that you struggle with sin is evidence that you *have* been saved. The spiritual battle points to new life. People who are dead in trespasses and sin do not feel the heavy weight of sin's guilt, power, and bondage. But saved people feel the struggle. As a pastor, I am not really concerned about the salvation of those who acknowledge the struggle against temptation. These faithful believers are fighting to overcome their sinful ways and desires by the power of Christ.

My concern is for those persons who profess saving faith in Christ, but they are content to live in a way that they know is disobedient to the commands of the Word of God. Galatians 5:16–17 issues the command, "But I say, walk by the Spirit, and you will not gratify the desires of the flesh. For the desires of the flesh are against the Spirit, and the desires of the Spirit are against the flesh, for these are opposed to each other, to keep you from doing the things you want to do." Indeed, every true believer is engaged in a real and continual struggle against sin.

But the good news is that you can live in victory over sin. No, I am not suggesting that you can achieve sinless perfection in this life. But you can experience true godliness, consistent obedience, and Christlike integrity. The Word of God found in Colossians 3:5-9 explains in powerful terms how to resist temptation and live in obedience to God. We must put to death what is earthly within us.

WHAT DOES IT MEAN TO PUT SIN TO DEATH?

Let's seek to understand this command to put sin to death by first clarifying what it does not mean. First of all, putting sin to death does not mean that you cover it up. Hiding your sin will only make you a good hypocrite. But it will not make you a godly man. Proverbs 28:13 explains, "Whoever conceals his transgressions will not prosper, but he who confesses and forsakes them will obtain mercy." Brothers, there is no such thing as a "secret sin." God knows all and sees all. Hidden sins on earth are open scandals in heaven. So while you may be able to fool other people in your life, you cannot hide from God. Our good God who won't let you down—won't let you off either.

David testifies, "For when I kept silent, my bones wasted away through my groaning all day long. For day and night your hand was heavy upon me; my strength was dried up as by the heat of summer" (Psalm 32:3-4). David learned the hard way that you can run but you cannot hide from God. He later learned, however, that you can run *to* God and hide *in* God! In verse 5 of that psalm, David testifies, "I acknowledged my sin to you, and I did not cover my iniquity; I said, 'I will confess my transgressions to the Lord,' and you forgave the iniquity of my sin." The Lord will do the same thing for you if you repent of your sins and run to the cross for forgiveness. First John 1:9 supports this truth. It promises, "If we confess our sins, he is faithful and just to forgive us our sins and to cleanse us from all unrighteousness."

Secondly, you cannot put sin to death by internalizing it. The God who sees your conduct also knows your heart. "For the Lord sees not as man sees: man looks on the outward appearance, but the Lord looks on the heart" (1 Samuel 16:7b). So you cannot please God or live victoriously if you quit a sinful habit but continue to embrace and entertain sinful desires. You must change your sinful ways and change your attitude toward sin entirely. You must clear away the cobwebs and kill the spider that created them. You must mop up the wet floor and turn off the overflowing faucet that caused it. You must deal with sin in your heart. Remember, the heart of the matter is the matter of the heart.

Proverbs 4:23–27 is wise instruction: "Keep your heart with all vigilance, for from it flow the springs of life. Put away from you crooked speech, and put devious talk far from you. Let your eyes look directly forward, and your gaze be straight before you. Ponder the path of your feet; then all your ways will be sure. Do not swerve to the right or to the left; turn your foot away from evil."

Lastly, you have not put sin to death just by replacing one sin with another sin. This is what King David did. David committed adultery with Uriah's wife. And Bathsheba became pregnant. But none of these experiences moved David to get right with God. Instead, David simply exchanged one sin for another to cover his tracks. And there was a free fall that led from adultery to deception, murder, and hypocrisy. Yet, after all of the hustling David did, he still was not able to get anywhere until he became honest with God.

David's failure warns us that you can't simply exchange one sin for another sin. Replacing homosexuality with pornography is not spiritual victory. Replacing adultery with masturbation is not spiritual victory. Replacing fornication with lust is not spiritual victory. These are all just attempts to avoid dealing with the real issues in our lives—the spiritual realities that exist underneath the skin. Brothers, we must put sin to death.

If putting sin to death is not accomplished by covering it, internalizing it, or replacing it, how do you put sin to death? First of all, you must hate sin passionately. It means that you establish a disposition of animosity toward your sin. The psalmist said: "Through your precepts I get understanding; therefore I hate every false way" (Psalm 119:104). That's how the process works in all of us. True spiritual understanding results in holy hatred for every false way. Note that the psalmist did not just hate the consequences of being on the false way. He hated the false way itself. In fact, he hated every false, evil way. He detested anything and everything that is contrary to the ways of God.

A little child was playing with a very valuable vase that he should not have even been touching. Of course, he put his hand into it and could not get it out. His father tried in vain to get the boy's hand free. His parents considered breaking the vase until the father said, "Son, let's try one more time to get you free. On the count of three, open your hand and hold your fingers as straight as you can, and then pull." To their astonishment the little fellow said, "Oh no, Daddy, I can't put my fingers out like that. If I do, I'll drop my pennies!" Now, let me ask you something. Are you asking the Lord to deliver you from some sinful ways while you are trying to hold on to the very things that have you bound?

Brothers, please recognize that you cannot cherish sin and kill it at the same time. You need to have spiritual animosity, godly ill will, and a holy hatred for sin. In fact, here is a practical way to begin to put sin to death in your life. Pray. Ask the Lord to teach you to love what He loves and hate what He hates. Sincerely and persistently pray, "Search me, O God, and know my heart! Try me and know my thoughts! And see if there be any grievous way in me, and lead me in the way everlasting!" (Psalm 139:23–24).

Secondly, putting sin to death means that you fight sin violently. The victory Paul is talking about here is military, not athletic. This is not a sport. It's a war in which we must fight to the finish. The Lord has graciously given us the whole armor of God for spiritual warfare. Our spiritual armor is described in Ephesians 6:13–17. However, you must know that the Lord will not fight the battle for you. You must fight for godliness in your life. This is the other side of sanctification. According to Philippians 2:12–13, God is at work in us to will and to do for His good pleasure. But we must work out our own salvation with fear and trembling. It is the will of God to have the Spirit of God use the Word of God to make the children of God look like the Son of God.

You and I have a role and a responsibility in this process. You can't overcome sin with a passive attitude that sits back and says, "Let go and let God." Spiritual growth does not happen through osmosis. You must take personal responsibility to deal with sin in your life. This responsibility does not lie just in the development of virtue; it's putting sin to death. Colossians 3:9–10 says, "Do not lie to one another, seeing that you have put off the old self with its practices and have put on the new self, which is being renewed in knowledge after the image of its creator." That's a great way to describe the process. You must take off the selfish ways of sin and put on the godly ways of Christ. You must pull up the weeds, then plant the flowers. You must walk in the newness of life that is described in Romans 6:3–4 and put to death what is earthly within you. That's the key to true godliness.

Brothers, we are in a war. And we should not deal with sin in a half-hearted manner. We cannot negotiate or compromise with sin. We must not treat the battlefield of faith as if it is a playground of life. If you are going to overcome sin, you must fight! You can't play with sin and think that sin will play nice and leave you alone! It won't. You must be aggressive, even militant, in battling your sins.

In Matthew 5:27–30, Jesus says, "You have heard that it was said, 'You shall not commit adultery.' But I say to you that everyone who looks at a woman with lustful intent has already committed adultery with her in his heart. If your right eye causes you to sin, tear it out and throw it away. For it is better that you lose one of your members than that your whole body be thrown into hell. And if your right hand causes you to sin, cut it off and throw it away. For it is better that you lose one of your members than that your whole body go into hell."

Of course, Jesus is not suggesting that dismemberment is the way to holiness. Amputating your hand does not fix a sinful heart. And gouging out your eyes will not cure you of lust. Jesus is graphically illustrating how aggressively, decisively, and militantly we must deal with sin. Jesus is stressing the point that whether you go to heaven or hell is infinitely more important than the use of your hands or the sight of your eyes.

So do whatever it takes to decisively attack sin in your life! You may need to cancel some magazine subscriptions or stop reading books that feed your flesh. You may need to quit some associations or develop new and different friendships. You may need to change some of your patterns at the workplace or even get another job. You may need to refuse to watch certain programs and movies or decide to not watch television at all. You've got to be willing to do whatever it takes to attack sin in your life!

Thirdly, you must deal with sin decisively. That's why there are no shortcuts to holiness. The laying on of hands is not a shortcut to holiness. Walking down an aisle is not a shortcut to holiness. You must fight to the finish. You must fight to gain and maintain spiritual victory. You must fight on your knees in fervent prayer. You must fight with the sword of the Spirit, which is the Word of God (Ephesians 6:17). You must fight alongside other godly soldiers who will support you and hold you accountable for your actions (Ecclesiastes 4:9–12).

First Samuel 15 records God's rejection of King Saul because of his disobedience. The Lord had commanded Saul to totally destroy the Amalekites. Saul apparently didn't understand that obedience is better than sacrifice. So he disobeyed the Lord's command, allowing the wicked king of the Amalekites to live, along with some other people and livestock. Consequently, the Lord rejected Saul as the king of Israel.

But there's an interesting conclusion to this story. Agag would not be spared because of Saul's disobedience. First Samuel 15:32–33 reports, "Then Samuel said, 'Bring here to me Agag the king of the Amalekites.' And Agag came to him cheerfully. Agag said, 'Surely the bitterness of death is past.' And Samuel said, 'As your sword has made women childless, so shall your mother be childless among women.' And Samuel hacked Agag to pieces before the Lord in Gilgal."

The prophet did what King Saul failed to do. He put Agag to death. Actually, he butchered Agag. He slaughtered him. He cut him into pieces. Moreover, verse 33 says that Samuel did it *before the Lord.* Consider that. Samuel did not view the hacking up of Agag as cruel and unusual punishment. He viewed it as an offering of worship to the Lord. Brothers, this is how we should view the call to self-mortification of our sinful ways. "I appeal to you therefore, brothers, by the mercies of God, to present your bodies as a living sacrifice, holy and acceptable to God, which is your spiritual worship" (Romans 12:1). Brothers, obedience to this call to worship requires that we hate sin passionately, fight sin violently, and deal with sin decisively.

WHAT SINS MUST BE PUT TO DEATH?

Ultimately, you must put to death any and every sin that threatens your devotion to Jesus Christ. The Lord Jesus desires, deserves, and demands our total devotion, absolute allegiance, and complete commitment. Brothers, we must not compromise at this point. Second Corinthians 7:1 offers: "Since we have these promises, beloved, let us cleanse ourselves from every defilement of body and spirit, bringing holiness to completion in the fear of God."

Some churches seem to think that if a man doesn't drink, smoke, sleep around, or commit other high-profile sins, he must be a godly man. But Scripture exhorts us to nurture holiness by dealing with both sins of the body and sins of the spirit. Hebrews 12:1 encourages us by saying, "Therefore, since we are surrounded by so great a cloud of witnesses, let us also lay aside every weight, and sin which clings so closely, and let us run with endurance the race that is set before us." We must take a stand against any sin that hinders our pursuit of godliness.

But more specifically, brothers, we must put sexual sin to death. Colossians 3:5 clearly states, "Put to death therefore what is earthly in you: sexual immorality, impurity, passion, evil desire, and covetousness, which is idolatry." This is the primary concern of the passage. We must put to death the sexual sins that burden our hearts with guilt, pollute our minds with trash, and hinder our souls from enjoying the fellowship with God that the bloody cross and empty tomb of the Lord Jesus have secured for Christians.

A certain pastor was leading the young adults in his church in a teaching session on sexual purity. During the question-and-answer time, one young man asked, "Pastor, why do all you preachers act like sexual sins are the worst sins in the world? You do know that there are other sins, don't you?"

The pastor graciously responded, "Son, you're right. Sexual sins are not the only sins. And they are not the worst sins. But, I put so much emphasis on them because you have to start somewhere. And I believe that if you can learn to practice self-control in this area, it would be a great head start toward learning to practice self-control in the other areas of your life."

I think the apostle Paul would agree. In 1 Corinthians 6:18, Paul teaches, "Flee from sexual immorality. Every other sin a person commits is outside the body, but the sexually immoral person sins against his own body." And here in Colossians 3:5, Paul exhorts us to put sinful sensuality to death. First of all, we must put to death the acts of sexual sin, which Paul refers to as "sexual immorality." The Greek word used here is generic, referring to all types of sexual sin. The point is that we must put to death every sexual sin because it is not in accord with God's will.

I think this is a good place to remind you that the act of sex is not sinful. God created sex. And God intends for sex to be enjoyed by one man and one woman within the

covenant of marriage. But any sexual activity that goes outside of that parameter is a sin that invites the judgment of
God. Hebrews 13:4 says, "Let marriage be held in honor
among all, and let the marriage bed be undefiled, for God
will judge the sexually immoral and adulterous." You have
to fight to put illicit sexual behavior to death.

But we must also put to death the desires of sexual sin.
Colossians 3:5 says that along with sexual immorality, we
must also put impurity, passion, evil desire, and covetousness to death. Here the term *passion* refers to uncontrolled
sensuality or undisciplined emotions. *Evil desires* refers to
desires that are set on wicked things. And Paul encouraged
the believers to also deal with covetous desires. Covetousness is more than greed. It's the unbridled desire for more.
And it usually focuses on that which is forbidden. Even
though we often associate covetousness with materialism, it
goes way beyond the desire for more stuff. Covetousness is
also manifested in our sexual desires.

The final word of the Ten Commandments is found in
Exodus 20:17, "You shall not covet your neighbor's house;
you shall not covet your neighbor's wife, or his male servant, or his female servant, or his ox, or his donkey, or anything that is your neighbor's." The Lord forbids the coveting
of your neighbor's house. He also forbids coveting your
neighbor's wife who lives in that house! So Paul wisely con-
veyed God's edict for us to put covetousness to death. Through
the Scriptures, he identified an important reason why we
cannot allow covetousness to live in our hearts: covetousness is idolatry. It is the worship of things.

Don't let anyone bluff you, brothers. Your god may not
be the God that you sing to and pray to on Sunday. Anybody can play church for a couple of hours on Sunday
morning. Your god is the thing that is most important to

you. Your god is the thing that you think about and desire the most. Your god is the thing that you value and treasure the most. It is idolatry when you allow the desire for illicit sexual fulfillment to become greater than your devotion to the Lord Jesus. Therefore, we must put to death the sexual sin—both the desires associated with it and the activities that result from it.

WHY MUST YOU PUT SIN TO DEATH?

There are four fundamental reasons why we must put sin to death. First of all, brothers, we must put sin to death because the Word of God commands it. This is a simple, but sufficient, reason for us to declare holy war on sin in our lives. We are compelled by the God-breathed Scriptures to put sin to death. But don't think of this biblical command as some burdensome obligation. Consider it a wonderful opportunity. The fact that the Word of God commands it means that you *can* put sin to death. Isn't that good news? You don't *have* to sin. God's commandment is God's enablement. Your life does not have to be defeated and dominated by sin. Psalm 119:11 says, "I have stored up your word in my heart, that I might not sin against you."

The second reason we must put sin to death is because the nature of sin demands that we put it to death. First Peter 2:11 offers wise counsel, "Beloved, I urge you as sojourners and exiles to abstain from the passions of the flesh, which wage war against your soul." Did you get that? Sin is not your friend. It is a mortal enemy that wages war against your very soul. Do not play with sin. Put it to death.

The third reason why we must put sin to death is found in Colossians 3:6, "On account of these the wrath of God is coming." First John 4:8 rightly declares that God is love.

But we must understand that the love of God is not some sentimental or emotional disposition that causes God to tolerate our sinfulness. Our God of love is also a God of wrath. That is, God is holy. And the holiness of God requires that sin be punished. In fact, if God allowed sin to go unpunished, His own holiness would be compromised. Therefore, the holiness of God necessitates the wrath of God.

Now, be clear that the wrath of God is not to be confused with the wrath of man mentioned in Colossians 3:8. God is not some temperamental God who flies off the handle when He is offended. Rather, our God is long-suffering, full of compassion, and slow to anger. But if you are slow to repent of your sins, God's slow anger will eventually catch up with you. The wrath of God is simply God's righteousness reacting to man's unrighteousness.

John 3:36 proclaims that, "whoever believes in the Son has eternal life; whoever does not obey the Son shall not see life, but the wrath of God remains on him." Romans 1:18 speaks further, "For the wrath of God is revealed from heaven against all ungodliness and unrighteousness of men, who by their unrighteousness suppress the truth." The wrath of God is coming. This does not mean that you can somehow lose your salvation. That's impossible. As believers, we have already passed out of death to life through Christ. We will not face that great day of God's impending wrath. We are eternally secure through faith in the person and work of Jesus Christ.

Then what is Paul saying here? Are we off the hook? Can we live any way we choose because we are saved by grace? Paul's response to this question is found in Romans 6:1–2 where he boldly declares, "By no means!" Brothers, our lifestyles ought to reflect our new life in Christ. We should put away the sinful ways that invite the judgment of God's

holy wrath. Don't be fooled. Sin always has negative consequences.

In fact, another helpful way to put sin to death is to
maximize the consequences of your sin in your thinking. As
weird as this may sound, the fact is that sin is pleasurable.
Let's be honest, brothers. You can have a lot of fun living in
sin. And that's exactly what sin offers us—pleasure without
consequences. The world says, "Have a good time! Do your
own thing! Live it up!" But the vital part of the story that is
tragically omitted is the fact that every sinful choice brings severe consequences. You cannot have one without the other.
Think about it. You can choose to jump off the roof of a tall
building. But after you jump, you're really out of choices. You
just have to deal with the consequences!

We live in a day when tens of thousands of people die in
America each year from sexually transmitted diseases. Yet
the best advice the world has to offer is to practice safe sex,
wear a condom, and get tested before you have sex with a
new partner. This is absolute foolishness! Sexual immorality comes with severe consequences. There are serious physical consequences. More importantly, there are inevitable
and unavoidable spiritual consequences. Galatians 6:7–8
asserts, "Do not be deceived: God is not mocked, for whatever one sows, that will he also reap. For the one who sows
to his own flesh will from the flesh reap corruption, but the
one who sows to the Spirit will from the Spirit reap eternal
life." This passage paints a haunting picture of the ironic
consequences of sin.

Paul says that if you sow to please your sinful desires,
you shall reap the corruption of the flesh by the flesh. Did
you get that? If you live to satisfy the desires of your flesh,
your flesh will turn on you and destroy your life. The same
flesh that tells you that God won't care if you do it will later

tell you that God won't forgive you because you did it. The same flesh that tells you to live as though it doesn't matter will contract a disease that kills you because you "had to have her." Sin will take you further than you want to go. Sin will keep you longer than you want to stay. And sin will cost you more than you want to pay. To avoid sin, you must magnify the consequences of sin.

Finally, we must put sin to death because the grace of God has already come. The list of sexual sins Paul gave in Colossians 3:5 was very specific. He warned in verse 6 that we must put them to death because "on account of these the wrath of God is coming." Then in verse 7 he adds, "In these you too once walked, when you were living in them." Brothers, we should put sin to death as we remember the sinful past from which the Lord has saved us.

In 1 Corinthians 6:9–11, Paul inquires, "Do you not know that the unrighteous will not inherit the kingdom of God? Do not be deceived: neither the sexually immoral, nor idolaters, nor adulterers, nor men who practice homosexuality, nor thieves, nor the greedy, nor drunkards, nor revilers, nor swindlers will inherit the kingdom of God. And such were some of you. But you were washed, you were sanctified, you were justified in the name of the Lord Jesus Christ and by the Spirit of our God." Before we met Christ, we were all on a collision course with the wrath of God. But in Christ we have new life.

In Titus 2:11–12, Paul teaches us the reason why we can turn our backs on sexual sin: "For the grace of God has appeared, bringing salvation for all people, training us to renounce ungodliness and worldly passions, and to live self-controlled, upright, and godly lives in the present age." The grace that saves us gives us the power to say no to sin.

By God's strengthening and sanctifying grace, we can put sin to death.

CONCLUSION

As a certain man rummaged about in a garage sale one Saturday morning, a partially concealed item caught his eye: a Harley-Davidson motorcycle. Because of its poor condition, the man was able to buy it for thirty-five dollars. After a few weeks, the buyer decided to work on the damaged bike. He called the dealership to inquire about parts. When he gave them the serial number, they put him on hold for what seemed to be an eternity.

Upon returning, they asked for his information and promised to call him back. The head of the dealership called back, instructing him to look for something under the seat. He did and found these two words inscribed there: "The King." He reported what he discovered to the head of the dealership, who immediately offered him $300,000 for the bike. A day later, a representative of Jay Leno from *The Tonight Show* called. Leno had heard about the bike and offered him half a million dollars for it.

You've probably caught on already. That bike did indeed belong to the king—"The King of Rock 'n' Roll"—Elvis Presley. Because of its condition, the bike was only worth thirty-five bucks. However, because of its ownership, it was worth at least half a million dollars.

Brothers, sin has left our lives in a bad condition. But if you belong to the King of kings and Lord of lords, your worth is immeasurable. No matter what your condition is, God can fix you up! God can restore your life! God can give you victory over you sinful ways!

Brothers, we must put to death any and every sin that

hinders our ability to honor God. We must do this because the Word of God commands it, the nature of sin demands it, because the wrath of God is coming, and because the grace of God enables us. We must commit to hating our sin with passion and fighting it with resolve. Knowing that we belong to the King, who alone can give us victory, should give us the confidence we need to wage war on our sexual sins and win. Let's start now and put our sexual sins to death.

➡ POINTS OF REFLECTION

1. What specific sins do you need to put to death in your life?

2. What practical biblical steps can you begin now to put sin to death in your life?

3. Who can or cannot help you maintain these practical biblical steps that will begin to put these specific sins to death?

4. What is going to be the hardest part of implementing the aforementioned steps? What are you going to do to subdue these difficulties?

5. Are you willing to take the necessary steps to put sin to death in your life? Why or why not? If not, explain your answer.

TRAINING OUR SONS TO OVERCOME SEXUAL TEMPTATION

⬆ A Battle Plan for Discipling Sons to Pursue Purity

2 Timothy 2:22; 3:10–17

— Pastor Brian Kennedy

IT'S eight o'clock Monday morning. You're dropping your son off to school, and as he walks through the gates, the girls start coming his way. You think to yourself, *They sure are dressed differently than back in my day.* You're running late, but your curiosity has been sparked. You decide to stay and observe for a moment. As you watch, you see and hear how the girls interact with your son, and then you see and hear how he responds to them. You get concerned for a moment and think to yourself that you need to have "the talk" with him, but then you push that thought out of your mind, telling yourself, *Aw, but he's so young.* You justify postponing the big discussion about sex again, thinking that when you were his age, nothing ever happened, no matter how hard you might have tried.

Let me ask you a couple of questions. Do you really believe that you just dropped your son off into the same world you grew up in? And as you look around, do you really believe that young men today don't need to hear "the talk"? Brothers, if so many of us struggled as young men to stay pure (and some of us are still struggling), then don't we all the more have to commit ourselves to equipping our sons so they can resist sexual temptation? We must prepare them, especially since we know that promiscuous sex has the power to endanger their lives and even their souls (Proverbs 7:24–27; Matthew 5:27–30). Brothers, we need to get over the awkwardness of having real talks about sex with our sons.

In some ways, it seems unnecessary to harp on how sex-crazed the world of our sons may be—because it is so obvious. All of the chapters in this book have already revealed a long list of sexual snares with which Satan has filled our world. But let me restate the obvious anyway: this is the time to reset the focus of this book on helping you to help your son. And in order to do that, we need to examine how the world really is for him. In his twenty-first-century world, through a whole assortment of electronic gadgets, he is connected to the good, the bad, and the ugly of this whole wide world. Furthermore, he is connected to his world 24/7. So when you think he is quietly studying or resting in bed, he very well could be busy teleconferencing with friends or even people you don't know. In addition to that, his text messaging activity goes on all day; for the most part it is unnoticed—no matter how alert you are.

Then there is the matter of how easy it is for him to access sex on almost any of his mobile devices. Sex comes at him on all sides, through virtually every form of media and entertainment, and his culture thinks nothing of it. It is a normal part of everyday life. In fact, in his world, having sex is actually a rite of passage that merits a sense of accomplishment, especially if you experience it early—*real* early. So don't think because he's young he doesn't know anything. Some twenty-first-century nine-year-olds could school you about some birds and bees that you never knew existed. They learn it from X-rated movies that they've seen on their TVs in the privacy of their bedrooms, streaming video clips they've found surfing the Internet, their worldly wise friends, or their friends' older siblings who are striving to live out the fantasies they pick up from watching music videos.

Now, perhaps in your day a teen had to hide in the trunk of an older friend's car to sneak into an X-rated drive-in movie. And even then, he'd only see a fraction of what is on your son's smartphone, a device that allows him to access porn anywhere at anytime.

On the other hand, you also know what sexually aggressive behavior eventually led to, even in your day. So you want to warn your son against pursuing girls like he's a Casanova. But if you came at him like that, he would probably respond: "Dad, when I walked out of the gym today, a young lady stopped me and asked if I wanted her. Getting girls these days is easy. I don't call *them*, they call me. Even some of the girls in church just walk up to us guys and get in our face. People think that we are always chasing the females, but that's not always true; they chase us too." Wow! At church? That's just a small slice of the sexually charged world that our sons live in.

Even if this captures only part of their world, then shouldn't our response be to try to steer them clear of the minefields of sexual temptation? We should all be doing something to help them withstand the Devil's intensifying, calculated attacks on their sexual innocence (John 10:10; Ephesians 6:10–12; 1 Peter 5:8). We should be working hard to save the hearts and futures of our sons from the pervasive decadence of a generation that is spinning aimlessly out of control. Knowing that the Scriptures give us hope and help in equipping our sons to walk in purity, the question we should seek to answer from the Word of God is: what is that something that we can and should be doing?

In one word, brothers, the battle plan that the Bible calls us to implement is called *discipleship*. This is the counterattack that God prescribes to fathers and men in the church to ward off Satan's assaults on our sons' purity. We are compelled to engage our sons in an ongoing empowering discipleship relationship. This chapter will give you the crucial discipleship principles that you need to start implementing in your relationship with your son in order to help him pursue purity with passion.

START YOUNG

In both the Old and New Testaments, the Word of God calls parents to start training their children from the moment they can understand the Bible. Solomon reported on the training he received from his father, David:

> *When I was a son to my father, tender and the only son in the sight of my mother, then he taught me and said to me, "Let your heart hold fast my words; keep my commandments and live; acquire wisdom! acquire understanding! Do not forget nor turn away from the words of my mouth. Do not forsake her, and she will guard you; love her, and she will watch over you." (Proverbs 4:3–6)*

The New Testament shows that even when faithful mothers and grandmothers have to fulfill the primary role of training their sons in the Word of God, God will bless their labor. In a very encouraging example for many in our community, the Bible records how a mother and a grandmother raised one of the pillars of the early church, the apostle Paul's apprentice, Timothy. Regarding the training Timothy received from those God-fearing women, the apostle Paul exhorted Timothy:

> *You, however, continue in the things you have learned and become convinced of, knowing from whom you have learned them, and that from childhood you have known the sacred writings which are able to give you the wisdom that leads to salvation through faith which is in Christ Jesus.* (2 Timothy 3:14–15)

Timothy was given some valuable life principles as a child that he wisely carried into adulthood. The word *continue* in verse 14 means "to stay in a place; to hold out; to stand fast; to stay still."[1] Paul commands Timothy to continue practicing the principles that he was given when he was coming up. The process by which Timothy learned the truth is critical for us to grasp. The truth was not only taught to him but it was also modeled.

Notice the major benefits in verse 14 you can reap if you start teaching your son when he is young and then faithfully continue to teach him throughout his upbringing:

◆ Your son will acquire a Christian worldview. The word *learn* means to direct one's mind to something.[2] It means to gain information as the result of instruction, whether in a formal or informal context; it means to be taught.[3] Your son will learn to see life from the biblical perspective that you teach to him.

- Your son will grow into a man with deep convictions. The word *convinced* means to be firmly persuaded of; to be assured of.[4] If you start when he is young and continue teaching him the Scriptures, you will be able to teach your son that the Bible is absolute truth. Through you, he can come to revere the Word of God and trust it to be accurate, authentic, and inspired by God.

- Your efforts to teach him the Gospel will empower him to reject the secular humanists' attempts to discredit the Scriptures. They claim that there is no absolute truth and that human reasoning supersedes the authority of God's Word. Through teaching him the Word of God, you will empower your son to resist the secular humanists' appeal for him to reject God and to live a self-directed life. What a terrible thing it would be if your son rejected God and refused to submit to the lordship of Jesus Christ.

- You will earn the starting spot in your son's heart as his trusted teacher. How much effort should you put into this process of teaching and modeling the truth to him? You must put in everything it takes to win the place of being his primary role model. When God opens the door for you to play first-string in his life, jump off the bench and hustle! Don't walk! Run onto the field and consistently work hard with your son as often as you can! Increase your skills to mentor him by spending time in prayer, studying the Word, and learning from others.

- Note that you can share some playing time with other godly role models. But do everything that you can, through the power of the Holy Spirit, to keep the starting spot in your boy's heart! Imagine that you—not popular culture, his friends, and strangers in chat rooms on the Internet—will be his trusted counselor who will answer the questions of life for him. There is no greater joy than knowing that you played the key role in helping your son to walk in the truth (3 John 1:4). Brothers, make whatever sacrifice you must to win that role. Satan and the world won't just give it to you. You have to fight, and fight hard, to win it.

The point is to start wherever you are, but start young whenever you can. Fritz Rienecker notes that it was the Jewish parents' duty to teach the law when their children were five years old.[5] What was Timothy taught? What was the curriculum? In 2 Timothy 3:15, we learn that Timothy was taught the sacred writings. Timothy was taught the Word of God when he was a child. If this seems like an overwhelming task for you, let me simplify it for you. Start off with the basics, and as your son grows over time, you will grow in your ability to take him deeper into God's Word. Let me give you a starting point followed by more principles that you need to apply in discipling your son (or another young boy or man in your church).

MAJOR ON THE MAJORS

Vince Lombardi, the Hall of Fame coach of the Green Bay Packers, was known for getting to the heart of the matter. His first interaction with the Packers as head coach began like this, "Gentlemen, this is a football." He began with the basics and continually emphasized the importance of getting "this football" into the enemy's end zone. He stressed that this was to be their primary focus.

In similar fashion, George Barna discusses the idea of raising "successful" children in his book entitled *Revolutionary Parenting*. He makes the case that we are using the wrong measures to determine our children's success.[6] He notes that the common measures we use for gauging the success of our parenting are whether or not they are

- provided with their basic needs: food, clothing, shelter,
- physically healthy,
- performing at or beyond their grade level,
- protected in a secure and comfortable home,
- monitored and cared for by parents,
- involved with church services and programs,
- connected to decent friends,
- not involved in gangs,
- not taking drugs,
- not alcoholics,
- not out-of-control sexually,
- not involved in a cult or in satanic activity,
- not the victim of physical or emotional abuse, or
- without a criminal record or related problems.

Many people, including Christians, use this list as the primary measure for determining their children's success. But, does God use this same list? He doesn't. Contrary to the world, the Scriptures define success in terms of one's relationship with God (Jeremiah 9:23–24). God's priority for both children and adults is to obey the greatest commandment: to love the Lord with all their heart, soul, mind, and strength (Mark 12:28–30). We must diligently teach our sons that loving God must be their highest priority and the most significant goal they pursue in their lives.

Do you want your sons to be successful? Then raise

them up to love God, to love the Word of God, to obey the Word of God, and to serve God. In Deuteronomy 6:4–9, God commands His people to train their children to recognize Him as their God and to love Him first with everything they have (heart, soul, and might). You must teach your sons to love God more than sports, more than girls, more than entertainment. You must teach them to love God more and their "entertain me," sex-crazed culture much less.

Adjusting your primary priorities to reflect God's desires must be the basis for your hope to successfully raise your sons to be sexually pure. God's way is superior to anything that we can think or imagine. Doing things God's way is our demonstration of love and obedience toward Him. Doing things God's way positions our sons to enjoy God's definition of success, God's favor, God's clear direction, and an intimacy with God which has the power to completely satisfy their souls (Joshua 1:8; Proverbs 3:1–8; John 14:21–23).

What happens when you faithfully teach your son the Scriptures and you focus on the majors; that is, knowing and loving God? According to 2 Timothy 3:15, learning the Scriptures gives our children the wisdom that leads to salvation through faith in Christ Jesus. The goal of childhood exposure to the Scriptures is to lead them to genuine salvation (v. 15b). In teaching your sons to love God, you must make sure that you teach them the only way it can be done. They must acknowledge their sin, turn from it in faith, and repent before God. They must trust Jesus alone for the salvation He grants by means of His death and resurrection.[7] Brothers, there can be no nobler task and greater privilege than to be God's ambassadors in preaching the wonders of the gospel to our sons and to lead them to the saving faith in Christ. So start young and major on teaching your son to love God and to embrace the gospel.

TEACH HIM THE TRUTH ABOUT SIN

I urge you to read through the book of Proverbs. There are thirty-one of them. Read one a day for one month and highlight in your Bible every time the wise father warns his son of the dangers of sin, particularly sexual sin (Proverbs 5:8; 6:23–24; 7:24–27). Men, if the very book in the Bible designed to teach fathers how to raise wise sons emphasizes telling your son about sin, then we most definitely need to teach our sons about sin in the world they live in. When you talk to your son, you don't have to tell him everything you know before he is ready to hear it, but you have to make sure that you prepare him for everything that he will encounter.

The following paragraphs chronicle the influences that he is most likely already facing.

The Centers for Disease Control and Prevention reports that by the time youth today finish the twelfth grade almost half of them have engaged in sexual intercourse.[8] Studies show that music is playing a major role in influencing illicit sexual behavior among our youth. Dr. Steven Martino of Yale Medical School, an expert in adolescent drug use and adolescent sexual behavior, recently published an article in *Pediatrics* about the effect that music with sexual lyrics has on the early onset of sexual behavior.[9] Note some of the highlights:

◆ Music with sexually explicit lyrics influences teenagers to engage in sexual intercourse earlier than those who do not listen to music with such lyrics.
◆ Sixty percent of teens, from ages fifteen to eighteen years, report spending one to three hours per day listening to music. Twenty-five percent listen for more than three hours per day.

- Some have even suggested that youth today cannot be understood without serious consideration of how music fits into their lives.[10]
- Youth who claim to listen only to the music and not to the lyrics are still impacted negatively due to the increasingly direct references to sex. "Magic Stick," by Lil' Kim is the example given in the study of such direct sexual content.[11]
- Sexual content is much more prevalent in popular music than through television, movies, magazines, and newspapers.
- The more sexually degrading the music they listen to, the more quickly teens progress in their sexual behavior, regardless of their race or gender. Sexually degrading music is characterized as portraying the male as an insatiable sex stud who pursues females exclusively as sex objects. The study used "Livin' It Up," by Ja Rule as an illustration of degrading sexual content.[12]
- Teens who watch videos with degrading sexual content by their favorite music artist, attend live performances of that artist, read related magazines, and expose themselves to the various messages of the artist, increase their advancement into sexual behavior.
- The more time teens spend listening to sexually explicit lyrics, the more likely they are to advance in their sexual behavior.
- Other underlying issues complicate the picture of young boys and teens engaging in premarital sex in today's culture.
- As the aforementioned study indicates, teens are going beyond exploration to sexual intercourse.

- Teens don't seem to question whether premarital sex is right or wrong. The abundance of adult portrayals of unbiblical sexual behavior gives youth a green light to follow suit.
- There is an explosion of overt sexual perversion around us. It is commonplace through television and music and easily accessible with smartphones, iPods, print media, porno shops, strip clubs, prostitution, sexually perverse fashion designs, and more.
- Some single parents are openly engaging in sexual activity right in front of their children and teens. (If you think that children are asleep or unaware of what you are doing sexually, you are hopelessly naïve.)
- Many married parents are having sex with people outside of their marriage. (Don't forget that kids today see more and talk more than you think.)
- Teens witness gay pride day at their public schools, and their homosexual and lesbian peers hold hands and kiss openly and proudly. The staff says nothing because on gay pride day no one can criticize or hinder the sinful activity of gay couples. Of course, heterosexual and bisexual students can then get busy, and if anyone says anything, they are quickly reminded of the freedoms that were allowed on gay pride day.
- The easy access to birth control and abortion for teens also raises the level of freedom to be sexually active.
- Young boys are assaulted with sexual temptation at every portal of the information highway (smartphones, MySpace, text messaging, TVs, CDs, and DVDs, written materials, to name a few). Sexual temptation is warfare at the highest level. The apostle Peter vividly describes how Satan will stop at nothing to devour anyone and all (1 Peter 5:8; 2 Peter 2:1–2).

Perversity is nothing new. It is older than Sodom and Gomorrah. Some two thousand years ago, Paul charged Timothy and the church to "flee from youthful lusts" (2 Timothy 2:22; cf., Titus 2:11–12). So the Bible is not silent about how to equip our sons to passionately pursue purity. In order to save their hearts, minds, and lives from the devastation of decadence in their world, we must teach them the truth about sin from the Word of God. The teaching we give them must be comprehensive. Telling them what to do is not enough. Telling them and then living out just the opposite of what we teach them is even worse. We must consistently teach them to discern sin, we must model godliness, and we must give them constant input.

The Word of God must be the daily bread we give to our sons. It is what will cause them to grow strong enough to overcome the daily battles for purity and overcome sin. Be encouraged. The Word of God tells us this goal is achievable. John declared, "I have written to you, young men . . . because you are strong, and the word of God abides in you, and you have overcome the evil one" (1 John 2:14).

SPEAK TO HIS HEART

Have you ever wondered about young men who have several children but are disconnected from them physically and appear to be disconnected emotionally? Have you ever wondered how the "baby's daddy" can pursue yet another lady, knowing that he is neglecting his existing responsibilities? And he does it with such cruel deceitfulness! How can he act like he has no attachments and live with himself? How can he continue to hurt another lady and lead her into a life of broken promises, abandonment, and even worse, the painful devastation of abortion? The heart is the issue!

Have you ever looked into the eyes of a coldhearted criminal? Whether they commit their crimes in government, in corporations, in churches, or on the streets, their eyes are the same. The coldness of their heart sends a darkening freeze into their eyes. The sparkle of love and the sanctity of life are absent, and their faces serve as frigid sockets that unwillingly mount cold eyes. The heart is the issue!

The heart is the inner self that thinks, feels, and decides. In the Bible, the word *heart* has a much broader meaning than it does in the modern mind. The heart is that which is central to man. Nearly all references to the heart in the Bible refer to some aspect of human personality.[13]

In Jeremiah 17:9, God says that "the heart is more deceitful than all else and is desperately sick." Brothers, you sin and your sons sin because we have sinful hearts. That's why you must use the Word of God to speak to your son's heart. His external sinful behaviors and internal attitudes are the result of his sin-producing factory—his heart (Genesis 6:5). The only way you can affect a permanent change in his behavior for the good is to apply the Word of God to influence a permanent change in his heart.

Therefore, you need to teach him how to guard his heart against the various issues he will confront in life (Proverbs 4:23). Sin, in particular, needs to be monitored and put in check, as needed. When you notice that your son's heart is losing sensitivity toward his siblings, toward you, toward other people and circumstances, put him on a spiritual heart monitor immediately. A sin-blockage has developed and needs to be cleared through the confession of sin and godly sorrow that will lead to genuine repentance (1 John 1:5–10; James 5:13–16; 2 Corinthians 7:9–10).

Avoid simply listening to words of apology from your

son. He may be telling you what you want to hear so that he can continue living a double life. Teach him to review his sin step-by-step and to feel remorse over it. In the first beatitude of Jesus' Sermon on the Mount, Jesus highlights our messed-up condition apart from God. Jesus says in the next beatitude, referring to those who grieve over their sinful condition, "Blessed are those who mourn, for they shall be comforted" (Matthew 5:4). God delights in those with a broken and contrite spirit.

Through the discipleship process, you must help him to "have a heart." You must teach him to feel the way God feels, to feel other people's pain, to have compassion and show compassion, as opposed to exploiting others.

In regard to sexual purity, we must teach our young boys to feel the loneliness, the pain of the past, the joy, the hopes and expectations in a young girl's heart. We need to teach them to show Christlike compassion, be a true friend, and help her out. Then they will respect, protect, and cherish young girls. They will also grow up to respect, protect, and cherish their girlfriends, wives, sisters, and daughters.

Helping our boys develop their hearts will help them to avoid committing cold and callous crimes against girls and women. It will also help our boys to no longer see getting young girls sexually the same as they see winning a sports trophy. They will no longer see themselves as "Mack Daddies" or "love machines," and they will begin to see young girls as either their sisters in Christ or as candidates for evangelism.

So in dealing with purity among our sons, we must also give special attention to the heart. In Psalm 119:9–11, you can see a picture of what will happen when a young man's heart cries out after God and he hides God's Word in his heart. When that happens the Spirit of God takes the Word of God, applies it to the child of God, and transforms him into a man of God.

TEACH THE WISDOM OF GODLINESS

The essence of biblical wisdom is learning how to choose the right paths which please God rather than the foolish ones which please only the flesh. In 2 Timothy 3:10-12, we find a unique insight for teaching our sons to discern the right paths. Here, Paul says to Timothy, his son in the faith, "Now you followed my teaching, conduct, purpose, faith, patience, love, perseverance, persecutions, and sufferings, such as happened to me at Antioch, at Iconium and at Lystra; what persecutions I endured, and out of them all the Lord rescued me! Indeed, all who desire to live godly in Christ Jesus will be persecuted." The key to finding the right path is following someone who knows where the right paths are. It's a lot like driving somewhere you've never been before. It really helps to follow someone who has already gone that way.

When you look at how Timothy followed Paul, you will notice that Timothy was not following the "bling-bling." Timothy was not following the party animals. Timothy was not following Paul to find all the women he could pursue in various churches, collect phone numbers, and try to be a missionary "Mack Daddy."

Timothy was young and single, so in traveling to many churches and being left behind by Paul to do follow-up work, he was faced with the same temptations that we are faced with today (1 Corinthians 10:13). Timothy had opportunities to become involved with the women, tamper with the money, hang with the wrong crowd, and indulge himself at the drinking parties.

Paul was Timothy's role model. According to 2 Timothy 2:22, Paul taught him to *run from* the people and the things that would hurt him and *run to* the people and things that would help him. He taught Timothy to say hello and good-bye to people who smiled in his face but would stab him in the back. Hence, Timothy learned to dismiss things that glittered but were not gold. He hung out with the right people —people who were following after God out of a pure heart (2 Timothy 2:22). That's the essence of teaching and learning wisdom.

What should we teach our young boys to expect when they choose to do things God's way? What should we teach our boys to expect if they choose to live a godly lifestyle and refuse to follow the hip-hop culture? What should they expect when they choose not to follow the gangsta rappers who are making millions of dollars portraying themselves as those who fearlessly live above the law? What should they expect when they choose not to follow those athletes who use their large sums of money to buy a lot of stuff and get in trouble with women, drugs, gambling, and all kinds of craziness? What should they expect when they do it right and choose godly role models as Timothy did?

Second Timothy 3:12 states, "Indeed, all who desire to live godly in Christ Jesus will be persecuted." Yes, on the one hand, all who live godly in Christ Jesus will suffer persecution. But, on the other hand, "godliness is profitable for all things, since it holds promise for the present life and also for the life to come" (1 Timothy 4:8). Furthermore, godliness is also "a means of great gain when accompanied by contentment" (1 Timothy 6:6).

Godliness is not popular in the world's eyes, but it results in happiness and fulfillment. Godliness is not popular in the world's eyes, but it helps our young men to make significant contributions in the world around them. Godliness is not popular in the world's eyes, but it helps our young men enjoy peace and sweet sleep when they close their eyes for rest (Proverbs 3:24). Godliness is not popular in the world's eyes, but it helps our young men enjoy success in God's way (Joshua 1:8). Godliness is not popular in the world's eyes, but it is pleasing in the sight of God.

UNDERSTAND THE KEY TO DISCIPLESHIP

Now, let me give you what seems to be the forgotten key to discipleship. It's not a magic program that you can buy from a Christian bookstore. It's not the latest fad coming out of the "we're the what's happening now church." You may not get it in the PowerPoint presentation of the popular new discipleship guru. The key to discipling your son is found in understanding how Paul made such a big impact on Timothy. It is grasping and doing what Jesus did with the Twelve. Every morning when you look in the mirror, you see the key to disciple your son.

The key to his discipleship is *you*. Discipleship—Jesus and Paul style—is to model the life that you want your disciple to follow. And while you are showing him how to live a life that pleases God, you patiently explain from the Bible what you are doing and why you are doing it. Paul said it this way, "Be imitators of me, just as I also am of Christ" (1 Corinthians 11:1). Mark described the Master's plan in his Gospel with these words, "He appointed twelve, so that they would be with Him" (Mark 3:14). Discipleship is the process of learning Jesus' ways. And through the power of the Holy Spirit, you must progressively yield every facet of your life to His authority in order to emulate Him.

To effectively disciple your son, you must become an effective disciple yourself. Becoming an effective disciple doesn't require a bunch of folks doing stuff for you. Jesus has done enough for you, and He has already given you enough. Brothers, seek Jesus. He will help you, and He really is all that you need (Philippians 4:13; 2 Peter 1:3). Becoming an effective disciple comes as a result of what you do, not so much what people do for you. What it boils down to is simply this, you have to love Jesus and live for Him in response to the way that He loves you. So it really does come down to what you will do for Jesus. You have a cross to carry and your life to yield to the Master. If you do that, then you will have a profound impact on your son.

Brothers, in so many words, that's the challenge of this book. It is a call to live like Christ, with Christ's power, for Christ's sake, and to influence your sons (and other young men under your influence) to live like Christ.

CONCLUSION

In conclusion, let me encourage you again that God's ways are always best, but a failure to follow them leads to disaster. In one of the most sobering accounts in the entire Bible, the book of Judges describes what happened to the generation of Israelites that came after Joshua and those who conquered the Promised Land along with him.

The people served the Lord all the days of Joshua, and all the days of the elders who survived Joshua, who had seen all the great work of the Lord which He had done for Israel. Then Joshua the son of Nun, the servant of the Lord, died at the age of one hundred and ten . . . All that generation also were gathered to their fathers; and there arose another generation after them who did not know the Lord, nor yet the work which He had done for Israel. (Judges 2:7–8, 10)

According to this passage, how long do you think it takes to lose a generation of young people to the world? The answer is the period of time for one generation to pass. That is stunning. After Joshua led the people into the Promised Land, the very next generation "forsook the Lord and served Baal and the Ashtaroth" (Judges 2:13). How is that possible? Brothers, there is only one way that could have happened. The parents didn't disciple their children in the ways of the Lord.

Isn't this at least in part why so many of our sons are turning away from God and His holiness to follow after the god of this world and sin? Brothers, if you don't want to lose your son, then don't procrastinate—implement a discipleship relationship with him now. Someone will train your son in sexuality; in fact, someone is doing so right now. The question is: is it you? I pray that it is you and that by implementing the biblical principles taken from this chapter, you will do it more effectively.

When I worked with Prison Fellowship, I often surveyed church congregations on the issue of one-on-one or small-group discipleship. It was typically a handful of people who were personally discipled one-on-one or in a small group after they gave their hearts to Jesus. My point is this: when it comes down to discipling an ex-prisoner, a child, or anyone else, the teacher frequently asks people to do something that he has not experienced himself.

Attempting to disciple someone without having first been discipled is awkward and ineffective. Yet discipleship still has to be done. Hence, we must get up to speed quickly and fulfill the command of Jesus to disciple (Matthew 28:18-20). Teaching our sons to observe all that we have learned in a structured discipleship training relationship is much better than sitting on the sidelines, hoping someone else will come along and do what God has called us to do.

Timothy is an example of what can happen when we pour our lives into the lives of our sons. Secular humanism and the sinful social practices around us are only going to intensify as time winds down (2 Timothy 3:1-9). Notice that the twin sins of idolatry and immorality did not stop Paul from walking with young Timothy, nor did idolatry and immorality stop Timothy from pursuing the things of God from a pure heart. Paul clearly modeled a godly life and Timothy obediently followed his example.

Brothers, through the power of the Holy Spirit, we must make young Timothys all over the world, starting first in our own homes. We must entrust the things of God to faithful young men who will be able to teach others also (2 Timothy 2:2). This is not a back burner issue or one that we can wait on for a few years. Young men are being targeted and pulled into sexual perversity every day. Can the church afford to lose another young man to sexual perversion? The answer is obvious, and the solution is obvious. The searching question that demands an immediate answer is: when will you get started?

POINTS OF REFLECTION

1. Do you understand the magnitude of the problem facing young men? If so, summarize the problem to another brother in less than five minutes. If you do not understand the problem, review the first part of this chapter and then summarize the problem to another brother.

2. Honestly review your Christian journey. Have you been discipled or are you in a discipleship training process? If yes, describe your discipleship training and compare it to what you see in the New Testament models (Jesus and His disciples; Paul and Timothy).

3. Do you have the starting spot as a role model in your son's heart? If you do not have a son, do you have the starting spot in the heart of a young man who needs a male role model? If you have the starting spot, explain how you earned it and how you plan to keep it. If you do not have the starting spot, what are you going to do to win it?

4. How closely do you monitor your son's heart? What specific steps do you take when you notice a sin-blockage in your son's heart?

5. When is it appropriate to discuss the challenges and benefits for young men that commit to living a godly life? Prepare a godliness challenge/benefit discussion and share it with the young man you are discipling. You are discipling a young person, right?

EPILOGUE: WINNING OUR SECRET SEX WARS

The Road to Reclaiming Our Purity

— Pastor Robert S. Scott Sr.

THE authors in this book have appealed to you in the previous chapters: (1) to stand on sound doctrine so that your mind and then your life can conform to purity, (2) to fear God when you are confronted with secret temptations, (3) to live according to the will of God, which is sanctification in sexual purity, (4) to learn that even godly men fall, so that you will better prepare yourself to war against the sexual temptations of pornography and adultery, (5) to live free from the slavery of sexual sin and instead to live, by God's grace, as slaves of righteousness, (6) to put sin to death before sexual sin kills you, and (7) to train our youngsters for purity and end the cycle of perversity that engulfs us. The only thing that remains to be communicated in this book is to encourage you one last time to do these things because God calls you to.

Some of you, no doubt, might feel that it's too late. Perhaps you've said to yourself several times while reading through this book, "I wish I had read something like this a year, five years, or even ten years ago, but now it's just too late." Let me encourage you that it's not too late to repent. Satan is a liar. And God, who cannot lie, says "If we confess our sins, He is faithful and righteous to forgive us our sins and to cleanse us from *all* unrighteousness" (1 John 1:9). That means, brothers, there is hope.

If God will forgive you, Romans 8:33–34 asks, then who is there who can condemn you? The question is, do you believe God will forgive you? If you do, then that faith will manifest itself in action. On behalf of all of the former slaves to immorality who are mentioned in 1 Corinthians 6:9–11, I plead with you to trust God's grace. He will not only cleanse you, but He will remove the shame of your guilt and return to you the joy of your salvation.

One of the most renowned men of God in all of history shared this truth in Psalm 51. He retells how God forgave him when he tragically fell in his secret sex war. This man is King David, and in bold, transparent words, he recounts for us (and the entire world) the path he took from the pit of enslavement to the road of reclaiming a life of purity.[1] We would all be wise to heed his instructions. He outlines four steps to recovery from sexual sin to liberating purity. And, brothers, you can be sure that this recovery program works because it is inspired by God!

STEP 1. PLEAD TO GOD FOR MERCY

David cries out to God, "Have mercy upon me, O God" (from Psalm 51:1, NKJV). If you have fallen, like David, in a secret sex war or are struggling to avoid one, then this is where you have to begin. You have to plead with God for mercy that you do not deserve. That is what mercy is. It is when God withholds from us what we deserve and instead gives us grace that we don't deserve. Reconciliation begins here. You must recognize your complete need for God—and God alone—to rescue you. He alone has the power to deliver POWs of secret sex wars, and He alone can heal mortal wounds of fallen warriors.

The Bible reveals in 2 Samuel chapter 12 that God sent Nathan to convict David of his secret sin. If the situation applies, I pray that we have been a Nathan to you and that you will respond as humbly as David did. For if you, like David, need to seek God's mercy, then like David, seek it according to God's lovingkindness. God's lovingkindness is His self-imposed obligation to remain loyal to all who humbly call out to Him for help.

Specifically, you must appeal, as David did, for God to erase His record of your sins. The picture in Psalm 51:2–4 is one of God keeping a written record of all of our sins. He is, therefore, the One to whom we must plead because He alone can wipe all our sins away. He is willing, if you humbly ask. Sinning against our loving Father is a grievous offense; yet, it is worse to reject His offer to wash away your sin with the precious blood of His own Son. Brothers, "'Come now, and let us reason together,' says the Lord, 'though your sins are as scarlet, they will be as white as snow; though they are red like crimson, they will be like wool'" (Isaiah 1:18).

On the one hand, sin stains us and makes us useless for God's service. On the other hand, with a heart full of compassion for sinners, Jesus proclaimed that He takes those who have been broken and worn out by sin and makes them useful to the Master again. The Scriptures tell of Him that "A BATTERED REED HE WILL NOT BREAK OFF, AND A SMOLDERING WICK HE WILL NOT PUT OUT, UNTIL HE LEADS JUSTICE TO VICTORY" (Matthew 12:20, emphasis original). This is good news, brothers. I pray that you will heed it and call out right now to God for mercy.

STEP 2. HONESTLY CONFESS YOUR SIN

Another key to recovering from falling in a secret sex war is confessing your sins. The antidote to secret sins is open confession. Brothers, David was forgiven because God is merciful and David *finally* confessed his secret sins. He prayed to God:

> *For I know my transgressions, and my sin is ever before me. Against You, You only, I have sinned and done what is evil in Your sight, so that You are justified when You speak and blameless when You judge. Behold, I was brought forth in iniquity, and in sin my mother conceived me.* (Psalm 51:3–5)

This is where all of the self-deceit, covering up, lying to others, twisting and leaving out facts must all stop. Give glory to God and honestly confess your secret sin, whether you think it is big or small. From Revelation 21:8, we know that the Bible is clear: the immoral and liars will go to the lake of fire. God requires everyone He releases from the power of sexual sin to fully confess their sins. By David's own mouth, he reveals what happens to us when we refuse to confess. You'll sink deeper and deeper into a morass of guilt as the psalmist describes in Psalm 32:3–5.

Instructively, all of the essential elements of true confession are present in Psalm 51:3–6. First, it states you have to acknowledge your sin. If you want to be a victor in your secret sex war, don't sugarcoat your sin anymore. If you are looking at porn, confess that you are committing adultery with your eyes. If you keep saying you are going to stop but you keep repeating that same old sin, then confess that you are enslaved to that sexual sin.

If you are emotionally and physically involved with a woman who is not your wife, call it fornication or adultery, and stop calling it love. You are defiling her and yourself, and love doesn't do that. The point is, no matter how hard it is to do, you must confess your sins. Think of how difficult it was for the king of Israel to confess his sins not only to God, but to publish what he had done so that it became a public confession to Uriah's family, Bathsheba's family, his own family, and the entire nation.

Several years ago, I had to make the hardest decision in my life. My eight-year-old daughter was diagnosed with a rare form of cancer, which most children weren't surviving. Her doctor asked me to sign a medical consent form that would authorize him to start my daughter on an experimental medical protocol. Before signing, he informed me that 10 percent of the patients didn't survive the first week of the treatment. He said that the treatment would cause excruciating side effects and could cause serious secondary diseases, including a rare life-threatening liver disease. And after all of that, he said the treatment would only boost her chances of survival by 20 percent.

I signed the consent form. I signed it, although I understood how horrific the treatment would be, because the consequences of not going through with it were worse. Without treatment she had a 100 percent chance of dying a torturous death.[2] Our choice was hard, but it was simple: suffer through the agony of the radiation and chemotherapy, or watch my daughter die without hope. Similarly, you have to choose to either suffer through the pain of confessing your sin or die spiritually as a slave of sin without biblical hope of forgiveness (see 1 John 1:8, 10). Treating sin is a lot like that, brothers. It takes radical spiritual surgery, called confession, to uproot sin from your heart, mind, and eyes. But in spite of the pain, you have to do it because God ordained it as the means to rid you of enslavement to sin. David and every other sinner delivered from immorality will tell you that freedom didn't come until confession did.

Second, acknowledge that your sin is against God. David says, "Against You, You only, I have sinned" (Psalm 51:4a). The truth is that all human offenses are, first of all, against God and not just against other human beings. As our Creator, it is God's laws we violate when we sin. So, even when our sin is against others, we are principally rebelling against God. Also, the very act of seeking things that God forbids is a direct way of implying that God has somehow failed to give us what we really need or deserve. Not only is that a lie, but it is a lie directed toward God.

Covetousness is the heart of sexual sins. Through it, we reject what God provides as if it isn't good enough, and we take for ourselves some form of sin as if it were better. God's response is given in Romans 1:24–27—when we reject Him and His ways (and choose instead to sin), He gives us over to a continual unsatisfying degrading passion for it. If, in this case, your sin is rejecting God to have forbidden sex, the obvious solution is to reject sexual sin to have God.

Third, allow God to use His Word to show you the depth of your sin. When David says, "Behold, I was brought forth in iniquity," the word *behold* is an interjection demanding attention. David uses it to place emphasis on what he says next. The convicting work of the Spirit had brought him to the shocking realization that he was the problem, and he had no one else to blame. God brings everyone who genuinely repents to this humble recognition. David exclaims, "Behold! I have been in a state of sin ever since my mother conceived me" (v. 5, paraphrase mine). To David's horror, for perhaps the first time in his life, he sees, "I really am this bad."

At this moment of honesty, he finally admits, "I have never been much better than who I am at this moment." He recognized that although he was an anointed man of God; that he had defeated Israel's great enemy, Goliath, when he was a mere boy; that he was Israel's most celebrated warrior; and that he was a great king; one fact never changed. He had the capacity to sin as gravely as anyone. So it matters not if you are a bishop, a pastor, a deacon, or anyone else in the church. Without God's enabling grace, you will fall straight on your face, lose, and keep on losing your battles to sexual temptation.

The problem is that we don't like that kind of honesty about ourselves. We are very good at deceiving ourselves. Jeremiah 17:9 attests to this truth. We will do almost anything, like David, to avoid confronting who we really are. Beware, brother. If you choose that route, then you have chosen the path that will take you deeper into your enslavement to sin.

STEP 3. PLEAD TO GOD FOR RESTORATION

Next, David pleads with God, "Purify me with hyssop, and I shall be clean; wash me, and I shall be whiter than snow" (Psalm 51:7). In so many words, David pleads with God to detoxify him of his once secret sins. He humbly petitions God to cleanse him from his sin, acknowledging that he could not clean himself. He even pleads with God to create in him a new heart. He longs to be cleansed from the inside out.

The word *create* in the Hebrew is used to describe God's miraculous work in Genesis 1 when He made everything out of nothing. David appealed to the Creator to take away his perverted heart and to replace it with an ethically clean heart. Under the conviction of the Holy Spirit, he realized that that is where his lust originated. He wanted a new heart so that he would love God more than the sins for which he lusted. He wanted a heart that would want what God wanted—namely, a heart that would, above all, thirst for God and His holiness.

But, for David, even that wasn't enough. He was afraid, as you should be, of falling back. So he asked God to "renew a steadfast spirit within [him]" (Psalm 51:10). He wanted God's enablement to be steadfast, firm, and permanent. He wanted to be a man of integrity. He didn't want to say that he loved God when, in actuality, he loved sin more. Brothers, the bottom line is that sexual sins, like all sins, are the results of our choice to love sin over God. David had been there, and he pleaded for God's presence to keep him from falling again.

What he wanted more than anything else was the intimacy he enjoyed with God. He knew that his sin was the reason why he experienced separation from God, and he knew that to continue in sin threatened a permanent loss of intimacy. So again, he cried out to the Lord: "Do not cast me away from Your presence and do not take Your Holy Spirit from me" (v. 11). This is what theologians call a *theocratic anointing*, which means God poured the Holy Spirit upon David to enable him to serve as king. This anointing is different than the permanent abiding gift of the Holy Spirit that new covenant believers receive at the point of salvation (see 1 Corinthians 6:19).

However, a theocratic anointing could be lost, as it was with King Saul (see 1 Samuel 16:14). David dreaded that reality more than the pain of confessing and letting go of his sin. So he chose to seek intimacy with God over illicit sexual intimacy with women. Brothers, that's the only way to have and enjoy the presence of God. You have to seek Him with all of your heart, and only then will He let you find Him. God won't compete with your secret lovers. He demands that you make loving Him your highest priority and your most important commitment. Jesus is very clear in Matthew 22:36–38 about who we should place first in our lives. Isn't this how He restored a guilt-ridden Peter after he denied Jesus three times? Jesus affirmed His love for Peter and three times solicited Peter's confession that the apostle loved Him. This heartfelt account is found in John 21:15–17.

STEP 4. RECOMMIT YOURSELF TO TRUE WORSHIP

In the end, the only true safeguard against falling in love with sexual sin is to possess a fervent love for God. I pray that having read this book, you know what David knew—that experiencing God's love is better than life itself. This is the sentiment that David expressed in Psalm 63:3. His soul longed for God and he humbly made this known in Psalm 42:1. When you unashamedly give your heart fully to God like that, brothers, then God will make Himself your greatest delight. And you won't be disappointed that you did.

Ask God for a heart to love Him more, and let Him have your sins—all of them. Love the true Creator of sex more than sex itself, and only then will you honor His gift and not pervert it by trying in vain to satisfy your lust. Here's the deal. Jesus offers to you, at the price of His life, His righteousness. What will it cost you? Absolutely nothing that is of any value. He wants to give you His righteousness in exchange for your secret sins—for all of your sins. Brothers, do the math. Don't be a fool. Repent today. I plead with you. Love your God. He will be your strength when you are weak. He will save you from any snare. But you must love Him more, yes, more, than your sexual sin.

Jesus said that you can only have one Master. You will love the one and hate the other as He explained in Matthew 6:24. You can't love both sin and God. In the Old Testament and in the New Testament, it is clear that true worship is serving God in obedient loyalty from a heart fully in love with God. In Psalm 51:10–19, David earnestly desired to have that closeness with God restored. God is seeking true worshipers. Has He found one in you?

One of my favorite biblical accounts is Jesus' encounter with the woman at the well. She was, by any measure, an immoral woman. The religious elite of her day despised her. Her own community rejected her. Her little secret sex sins weren't all that secret. Her life was a moral failure. That is, until she met a Man who told her everything she had ever done, until she met a Man who gave her living water, until she met Jesus the Christ, and until He made her a true worshiper (see John 4:3–42).

Brothers, Jesus is not done yet. He wants more worshipers. He said, "True worshipers will worship the Father in spirit and truth; for such people the Father seeks to be His worshipers" (John 4:23). He wants to mend broken worshipers. He wants to restore fallen ones. I pray that today you will let go of the fleeting pleasures of sin and let Him give you the everlasting delight of living as a true worshiper of God.

David concludes his appeal for God to make him a worshiper without hypocrisy. He refused to be content with performing the acts of external worship. Brothers, coming to church, singing in the choir, or teaching a Bible study won't be enough if your heart is still in another woman's bed. David said of God, "For You do not delight in sacrifice, otherwise I would give it; You are not pleased with burnt offering" (Psalm 51:16). Did you catch that? God won't delight in your doing the external things that you do unless they are accompanied by the fruit of repentance. The Word of God says God neither delights in that nor does it please Him. This is why going to church while living in sin is unacceptable worship to God.

What, then, does God desire? "The sacrifices of God are a broken spirit; a broken and a contrite heart, O God, You will not despise" (Psalm 51:17). Once you have offered God spiritual sacrifices of repentance and your heart is right, then God is pleased with literal sacrifices. David says of God, "Then You will delight in righteous sacrifices, in burnt offering and whole burnt offering; then young bulls will be offered on Your altar" (Psalm 51:19).

It is amazing that God turned a conniving, murderous adulterer into a fervent, jubilant worshiper. A grateful David declared God's praises in Psalm 51:15. If God transformed David, He can transform you. The question is, do you want that? Do you want His lovingkindness to mean more to you than life like David spoke about in Psalm 63:3? Do you desire it more than even pornography and illicit sex? Then plead to God, knowing that He can restore you, and plead to God, contemplating the alternative. God will not allow His gracious offer for forgiveness to be spurned forever.

Follow the example in Joshua 24:15 and choose today whom you will serve.

At the end of the day, brothers, the battle for purity hinges around a single issue—are you willing to whole-heartedly love God by obeying His Word? Unlike the lies we learn from our pervasive cultural images and icons that portray love as a romantic, erotic feeling, God defines love as obedience—pure and simple. Jesus said, "If you love Me, you will keep My commandments" (John 14:15). It is a choice, a life or death choice; a freedom or enslavement choice, God has left us in a world full of sin, and we have to choose if we will seek to enjoy it or Him. Jesus said it this way, "But so that the world may know that I love the Father, I do exactly as the Father commanded Me" (v. 31). Brothers, let your love for God show, and choose Him rather than the forbidden fruit of immorality.

As a minister called to preach the Word of God, I would be negligent to conclude this book without calling you to respond in obedience to God's Word. You have read a lot. No doubt, you have learned a lot. But this book isn't about giving you information for information's sake. This book was written with a passionate, urgent prayer from brothers with a burden to help brothers gain victory in their secret sex wars. We have labored in the Scriptures to try to persuade you that with God you can live a life of purity.

But this is as far as we can go. Now it's your turn to do something. If you are sinning in secret sexual ways, then like King David, you have to turn from it and confess it. I encourage you to reread Psalm 32 and Psalm 51 and pray them back to God in your own words. Then for each of the next thirty days, commit to reading and meditating on 1 Thessalonians 4:1–8. Count the cost and confess your sins to whoever has been affected by your secret sin.

Find someone who will pray with you and hold you accountable. Also, resolve to stop giving your flesh an opportunity to seduce you to sin. Rid yourself of everything that causes you to stumble. And write out a purity creed like Job did, one that you will abide by. Then give it to someone who will hold you accountable to it. Finally, love God, brothers. Love Him the same way that He loves you. If He has loved you with His best (and He has) then love Him back with yours.

A CONCLUDING PLEA

In one of the most critical junctures of World War II, Winston Churchill raised this battle cry to the leaders of Britain:

> I have, myself, full confidence that if all do their duty, if nothing is neglected, and if the best arrangements are made, as they are being made, we shall prove ourselves once again able to defend our Island home, to ride out the storm of war, and to outlive the menace of tyranny, if necessary for years, if necessary alone.
>
> Even though large tracts of Europe and many old and famous States have fallen or may fall into the grip of the Gestapo and all the odious apparatus of Nazi rule, we shall not flag or fail.
>
> We shall go on to the end, we shall fight in France, we shall fight on the seas and oceans, we shall fight with growing confidence and growing strength in the air, we shall defend our Island, whatever the cost may be, we shall fight on the beaches, we shall fight on the landing grounds, we shall fight in the fields and in the streets, we shall fight in the hills; we shall never surrender.[3]

The allies did persevere. They won an epic war over their German enemy. Brothers, if men fought with such resolve to save their physical lives and liberties, how much more should we resolve to fight against sin which can destroy our very souls. Our Commander-in-Chief calls us to battle. Let us, therefore, fully resolve, brothers, to win this war. Let us fight with our eyes, fight with our hearts, fight with our minds, fight against our flesh.

We must fight and continue to fight and never give up. We can win this war—through Christ our Lord. And we must commit to not leave a fallen brother on the battlefield. So brothers, what we need is a revival; that is, a revival in purity. And it can start with you. Right where you are. Right now. Heed the battle cry for purity and join the brothers, who by God's grace, are committed to living victoriously over secret sex wars.

May God help you to stand, and may His presence and grace abide with you and make you a victorious warrior for purity.

NOTES

Introduction

1. U.S. Attorney General, *Final Report of the Attorney General's Commission on Pornography*, 1986.

2. Reuters reported on Monday, February 16, 2006, that "of more than 2,500 university and college students polled across Canada, 87 percent of them are having sex over instant messenger, Webcams or the telephone," http://www.cnn.com/2006/TECH/internet/02/15/canada.sex.reut/index.html.

3. Safe Families is a morally safe one-stop source for the latest statistics on pornography. The STATS in this paragraph have all been taken from that site, http://www.safefamilies.org/sfStats.php (accessed October 2007).

4. Focus on the Family, *Pornography: Harmless Fun or Public Health Hazard?*, testimony by Daniel Weiss at the May 19, 2005, Summit on Pornography and Violence against women and children, https://www.family.org/socialissues/A000001158.cfm?eafref=1.

5. These statistics were taken from another safe and helpful site: http://www.blazinggrace.org/pornstatistics.htm (accessed October 2007).

6. Ibid.

7. Nowhere is this point more plainly demonstrated than in what is happening to many of the unplanned pregnancies occurring as a result of the rise in illicit sex. Clenard H. Childress documents the horrific fact that African American women are aborting their babies at unparalleled rates. I challenge every reader of this book to take a minute and soberly go through the web page http://www.blackgenocide.org created and launched by Pastor Clenard H. Childress. He contends that although African American women make up only 6% of the U.S. population, we should not boast a staggering 36% of all the abortions in the U.S.

Chapter 1: Slaying the Fiery Beast

1. *Sound* is from the Greek word *hugiainō*, from which we get our English word *hygiene*. It refers to that which is whole and in good health. Abbot-Smith, *Manual Greek Lexicon of the New Testament* (Edinburgh: T & T Clark, 3rd ed. 1994), 454.

2. *Discipline* is from the Greek word *gymnazō*, from which we get our English word *gymnasium*. It refers to rigorous exercise and training. Abbot-Smith, *Manual Greek Lexicon of the New Testament* (Edinburgh: T & T Clark, 3rd ed. 1994), 96.

3. Theologian Wayne Grudem defines sanctification as "a progressive work of God and man that makes us more and more free from sin and like Christ in our actual lives." Wayne Grudem, *Systematic Theology, An Introduction to Biblical Doctrine* (Grand Rapids, Mich.: Zondervan Publishing House, 1994), 746.

4. It is true that God's Word always accomplishes its sovereign purposes (Isaiah 55:10-11), but it is equally true that those who hear God's Word must exercise faith in it. The writer of Hebrews expresses this fact as he writes, "For indeed we have had good news preached to us, just as they also; but the word they heard did not profit them, because it was not united by faith in those who heard" (Hebrews 4:2).

5. Here is a list of representative texts corresponding to the truth claims presented in this section (Genesis 1:1, 26-28; 3; 6:5-7; Romans 2:8; 3:23; 5:12-14; Ephesians 2:1-3; Isaiah 64:6; John 8:34; Romans 5:10; 2 Thessalonians 1:9).

6. Here is a list of representative texts corresponding to the truth claims presented in this section (John 3:16; 1:1, 14-18; Matthew 1:21; Romans 3:23-26; 5:18; 2 Corinthians 5:21; Galatians 1:4; 4:4-5; 1 Corinthians 15:3-4; Acts 16:30-31; 17:30-31).

7. See Judges 13-16 for the complete story of Samson.

Chapter 2: Fearing God When No One Else Would Know

1. John Owen, *The Works of John Owen*, vol. viii, edited by Thomas Russell (London, U.K.: R. Baynes, 1826), 180.

2. Joannie Schrof, "A Sad but Essential Ingredient: The Lie—Adultery in America," *U.S. News and World Report*, August 31,1998, 31. In this brief article, Schrof concludes that the increasing instances of adultery are related to a lack of integrity in the American home. A telling example: 99 percent of Americans say adultery is wrong when it comes to their spouse, but "roughly 1 in 4 spouses—some 19 million men and 12 million wives—has had an affair."

   Lorraine Ali and Lisa Miller, "The New Infidelity," *Newsweek*, August 9, 2004, http://www.newsweek.com/id/54764 (accessed October 7, 2007). The subtitle reveals the heart of the article: "Overworked and underappreciated, more American wives are seeking comfort in the arms of other men." Ali and Miller uncover a rising trend of women who are seeking emotional and sexual fulfillment elsewhere. Two sobering realities: (1) Sixty percent of women find their partners at work; (2) Some data indicates that the trend is for women to equal men in the percentages of those who are unfaithful. See also: Lorraine Ali and Lisa Miller, "The Secret Lives of Wives," *Newsweek*, July 12, 2004, http://www.newsweek.com/id/54389 (accessed October 7, 2007).

   James Patterson and Peter Kim, *The Day America Told the Truth* (New York, NY: Prentice Hall Press, 1991). Patterson and Kim investigated the shifting moral, religious, and ethical climate of our country, and supplied substantial statistical data reflecting the changing landscape of our land. Chapter 12 (pp. 94-99): "Infidelity: It's Rampant in All Nine Regions" unveiled the sober reality that adultery was increasing even in the *Bible Belt*. A sampling: one third of married Americans had or were guilty of adultery; only 9 percent of men and 6 percent of women intend to marry their partners; love is not the issue: two-thirds of men and 57 percent of women said they did not love their partner; the New England states led in infidelity.

3. *Tyra Banks Show,* "The New Sex in the City" (October 22, 2007). This episode featured a panel of women with opposing views on sexual freedom. The majority of the panel included women who represented the new "sexually aggressive woman." One guest represented herself as "a strong black woman who will get what I want." And what she wanted was sex with as many men as she pleased. Women like those on the show are growing in number, and in some ways reflect the spirit of Potiphar's wife—I saw him and I wanted him.

   Paula Kamen, *Her Way: Young Women Remake the Sexual Revolution* (New York, NY: NYU Press, 2000). Written by a young feminist, who represents the new age of women who desire sexual freedom and control of their destinies. One telling excerpt from the book captures its flavor and goal to represent the "new woman." "While they may be similar to feminists because of their desire to take control of their own lives, superrats have absorbed the individualistic advances of feminism, such as sexual self-determination and control . . . For this reason, 'superrat' is probably most appropriate as an adjective describing the sexual assertiveness of this new generation, instead of a rigid academic category describing their complete personhood" (pp. 22–23). Throughout the book, Kamen examines various shifting attitudes of women and sex, and the numerous statistical accounts of this new expression—from the decreasing number of women who see virginity as a virtue, to what is acceptable in bed, the changing attitude of men toward aggressive women, and how women may have contributed more to legitimating the single life than men.

4. Dean Hamer and Peter Copeland, *The Science of Desire* (New York, NY: Simon & Schuster, 1995). This work was significant in beginning a watershed of dialogue over the issue of whether homosexuality is genetic.

5. *Dateline NBC*, "Your Cheatin' Heart: One Theory of Why Men and Women Have Extra-Marital Affairs," (February 7, 1995). When anthropologist Helen Fisher was asked by the Dateline reporter whether a person's cheating could simply be based on the person not "being a very nice person," Fisher's response said that it must be genetic because no one would sacrifice so much: "No, there's all kinds of psychological explanations for cheating, and they're all perfectly good, but why did he have a roving eye in the first place, this louse? I mean, most people really do not choose to sabotage themselves. I mean, when somebody is adulterous, they are jeopardizing not only their health and their life, because they could get AIDS, but they're jeopardizing their children, their spouse, their friends, their job, their money, their social status, their—even their conception of who they are. I mean, you loose a great deal by adultery, but yet, both men and women do it, not only in America but around the world." Fisher is right in that people risk and sacrifice a great deal when they commit adultery. However, Jesus was clear that adultery is *the choice of a sinful heart* and not a result of genetic makeup (Matthew 5:27–30).

Chapter 3: Living According to the Will of God

1. R. Kent Hughes, *The Disciplines of a Godly Man* (Wheaton, Ill.: Crossway Books, 1991), 23.

2. Solo-sex, sex with oneself, or self-stimulated sex should be viewed as a sexual sin and under the umbrella of sexual immorality. See Daniel R. Heimbach, *True Sexual Morality* (Wheaton, Ill.: Crossway Books, 2004), 222–23, for a biblical justification of this view.

3. The literature on this interpretive issue is vast. The discussions range from nontechnical to technical and can be found in a variety of resources including commentaries, journal articles, theses, dissertations, etc. For a nontechnical presentation of the views and the position advocated in this chapter, see John F. MacArthur, *1 & 2 Thessalonians* (Chicago: Moody Publishers, 2002), 106–107.

Chapter 4: Learning from Men Who Have Fallen

1. I am in no way trying to limit the definition of pornography to soft porn images of airbrushed female bodies. The majority of pornography today is anything but soft. It mirrors the degrading perversions that God warns against in Leviticus 18:6–30 (sins of child porn, incest, bestiality, etc.). It is my aim in this chapter to show you how dangerous a gateway drug soft porn can be. David saw nothing more than by today's standard a PG-13 movie; it enraged his lust and prompted him to take a woman and kill her husband to cover his tracks.

2. Robert L. Alden demonstrates that the term *garment* refers to Joseph's coat in Genesis 37:3, robes worn by priests in Exodus, Leviticus, and Ezra 2:69. It also is used to designate the robes worn by King David's virgin daughters in 2 Samuel 13:18–19 in *New International Dictionary of Old Testament Theology & Exegesis*, ed. by Willem A. VanGemeren [Grand Rapids, Mich.: Zondervan Publishing House, 1997], 2:742–43.

3. God gave mankind the charge to be fruitful, to multiply, and to fill the earth. To fulfill that commission, God also gave us a very strong sex drive. However, we have to resist the seemingly never-ending temptations from the world, our flesh, and Satan to misuse that drive.

4. The Barna Research Group reports that 38 percent of adults believe it is "morally acceptable" to look at pictures of nudity or explicit sexual behavior and use pornography, "Morality Continues to Decay," November 3, 2003, http://www.barna.org/FlexPage.aspx?Page=BarnaUpdate&BarnaUpdateID=152.

5. Focus on the Family, "Pornography: Harmless Fun or Public Health Hazard?" testimony by Daniel Weiss at the May 19, 2005 Summit on Pornography and Violence against Women and Children, https://www.family.org/socialissues/A000001158.cfm?eafref=1. Weiss cited research that demonstrated the progressive nature of pornography:

> Once addicted, a person's need for pornography escalates both in frequency and in deviancy. The person then grows desensitized to the material, no longer getting a thrill from what was once exciting. Finally, this escalation and desensitization drives many addicts to act out their fantasies on others. . . . At a Senate hearing last fall, medical experts . . . described research showing the similarity of porn addiction to cocaine addiction. Further, because images are stored in

the brain and can be recalled at any moment, these experts believe that a porn addiction may be harder to break than a heroin addiction.

6. I don't have space to discuss strengthening your marriage but Stuart Scott, *The Exemplary Husband: A Biblical Perspective* (Bemidji, Minn.: Focus Publishing, 2000) is an excellent resource to start with.

7. Of course this charge is overly simplistic. Getting married needs to be pursued with a lot of thoughtful wisdom, and you need to thoroughly prepare yourself before you ask someone the question, "Will you marry me?" On the other hand, brothers, there is a very concerning trend that single brothers are waiting longer and longer to get married. While that is happening, all of us are being exposed to more and more sexual temptations. That's a recipe for disaster. The bottom line is that first for the glory of God and for the purity of His people, single brothers, if you have strong sexual desires, you need to stop dragging your feet about getting married! To see some of the reasons why brothers aren't getting married check out, "Why Are Black Men Avoiding Marriage? Ask Former NFL Running Back Jerone Davison," http://www. blacknews.com/pr/spiritualfragranceofawoman101.html.

8. R. Kent Hughes, *Disciplines of a Godly Man* (Wheaton, Ill.: Crossway Books, 1991), 29.

9. While James is speaking primarily of spiritual death, it is worth noting that unyielding sin leads to physical death as well. In their monumental yet gut-wrenching report by the National Urban League and United Way of Los Angeles, "The State of Black America," April, 2005, http://www.nul.org/thestateofblackamerica.html determined that:

- Blacks have a far higher death rate than other groups at 979, followed by Whites at 700, Latinos at 540, and Asians at 445. Male death rates are much higher than females in all groups.

- Most dramatic are African American death rates from homicide and HIV/AIDS, more than three times higher than other groups, striking men particularly hard.

- Premature deaths rob African Americans of many years of life: their rate of 106.4 far outstrips that of Latinos at 43.4, Whites at 55.8, and Asians at 28.5.

- The teen death rate is much higher for Blacks due to high homicide rates, often gang related.

Chapter 5: Living Free from the Slavery of Sexual Sin

1. Millard J. Erikson, *Christian Theology* (Grand Rapids, Mich.: Baker Books, 1998), 534-35.

We experience full humanity only when we are properly related to God. No matter how cultured and genteel, no one is fully human unless a redeemed disciple of God. This is the human *telos*, for which they are created. There is room, then, in our theology for humanism, that is, a Christian and biblical humanism that is concerned to bring others into proper relationship with God. The New Testament makes clear that God will restore the damaged image, and perhaps even build upon and go beyond it (2 Corinthians 3:18).

2. *New Webster's Dictionary and Thesaurus*, 1991, 357.

3. Centers for Disease Control & Prevention, "Fact Sheet: HIV/AIDS among African Americans," http://www.cdc. gov/hiv/topics/aa/resources/factsheets/aa.htm, revised June 2007.

4. Bridget E. Maher, "Abstinence Until Marriage: The Best Message for Teens," http://www.frc.org/get.cfm?i=ISO3B1.

5. "Abstinence-Only-Until-Marriage Programs: Ineffective, Unethical, and Poor Public Health," http://www.advocatesforyouth.org/PUBLICATIONS/policybrief/pbabonly.htm.

Virtually all Americans have sex before marrying—a fact that has been true since the 1950s. The unrealistic, morality-based agenda that abstinence-only programs are attempting to promote runs counter to the life choices of almost all Americans. The present median age of sexual initiation is 17 and the average age of marriage is 25.8 for women and 27.4 for men, meaning that the length of time between sexual onset and marriage is 8 to 10 years on average. The gap between sexual onset and marriage has increased across time and premarital sex is an almost universal practice. By age 20, 75 percent of Americans have had sex before marriage; the percentage rises to 95 percent of Americans by age 44. Even among those who abstained from sex until age 20 or older, 81 percent have had premarital sex by age 44.

Abstinence-only-until-marriage programs are of little value to sexually active teens and, by definition, discriminate against lesbian, gay, bisexual, and transgender youth. Adolescents are often reluctant to acknowledge sexual activity, seek out contraception, and/or discuss sexuality, even in the most open settings. Abstinence-only programs do not provide a much-needed forum in which sexually active adolescents can address critical issues—such as safer sex, the benefits of contraception, legal rights to health care, and ways to access reproductive health services. Instead, abstinence-only programs allow discussions only within the narrow limits developed by conservatives in Congress.

Promoting marriage as the only acceptable family structure denigrates the choice of many Americans to be single or live in nontraditional arrangements. Despite the message of abstinence-only-until-marriage programs that marriage is the expected standard of human behavior, individuals should have the right—without governmental interference or proselytizing—to determine if and/or when marriage may be an appropriate or desirable life choice. The number of Americans who are unmarried and single has been growing steadily in recent years, reaching 89.8 million in 2005, and including 41 percent of all U.S. residents age 18 and older. In 2005, 55 million households were headed by unmarried men or women—49 percent of households nationwide; and 12.9 million single parents lived with their children. Nearly 30 million people lived alone (26 percent of all households), up from 17 percent in 1970. Forty percent of opposite-sex, unmarried-partner households included children.

6. "Adolescent sexuality in the United States," http://en.wikipedia.org/wiki/Adolescent_sexuality_in_the_United_States.

7. St. Augustine, "Confessions of St. Augustine," vol. 1, *Believer's Bible Commentary* (Nashville: Thomas Nelson, 1995), 878.

8. C. S. Lewis, "Letters to an American Lady," *New Bible Commentary*, 28, www.sermonillustrations.com/a-z/h/holy.htm.

9. Phillip Brooks, *Perennials*. www.sermonillustrations.com/a-z/f/freedom.htm (accessed November 24, 2007).

Chapter 6: Putting Sin to Death

1. All Scripture in this chapter is taken from the English Standard Version (ESV).

Chapter 7: Training Our Sons to Overcome Sexual Temptation

1. Gerhard Kittel and Gerhard Friedrich, eds., *Theological Dictionary of the New Testament* (Grand Rapids, Mich.: William B. Eerdmans Publishing, 1985).

2. Ibid.

3. Ibid.

4. Joseph Thayer, *Thayer's New Greek-English Lexicon on CD-ROM*, Biblesoft, PC Study Bible Version 4.1B, 2003.

5. Fritz Rienecker and Cleon Rogers, *Linguistic Key to the Greek New Testament* (Grand Rapids, Mich.: Zondervan Publishing House, 1976).

6. George Barna, *Revolutionary Parenting* (Carol Stream, Ill.: Tyndale Publishing House, 2004).

7. For a fuller presentation of the Gospel refer to Anthony Kidd's explanation of the Gospel in chapter one, pages 25–27.

8. U.S. Centers for Disease Control and Prevention, "Youth Risk Behavior Surveillance," *Morbidity Mortal Weekly Report*, May 21, 2004, <http://www.cdc.gov/mmwr/PDF/ss/ss5505.pdf>. showed that

nationwide 46.7% of students had sexual intercouse during their lifetime. The prevalence of having had sexual intercourse was higher among black male (73.8%) and black female (60.9% students than other students.

9. Steven C. Martino and others, "Exposure to Degrading Versus Non-degrading Music Lyrics and Sexual Behavior among Youth," *Pediatrics* 118, no. 2 (August 2006), doi:10.1542/peds.2006-0131, http:// pediatrics.aappublications.org/cgi/content/full/118/2/e430 (accessed October 15, 2007).

10. Peter G. Christenson and Donald F. Roberts, *It's Not Only Rock and Roll: Popular Music in the Lives of Adolescents* (Cresskill, NJ: Hampton Press, 1998).

11. Lil' Kim, "Magic Stick," on *La Bella Mafia* CD (New York, NY: Atlantic Records, 2003).

12. Ja Rule, "Livin' It Up," on *Pain is Love* CD (New York, NY: Def Jam Recordings, 2001).

13. *Nelson's Illustrated Bible Dictionary* (Nashville: Thomas Nelson Publishers, 1986).

Epilogue: Winning Our Secret Sex Wars

1. The superscription that appears in your Bible before verse one is actually a part of the Hebrew text. It gives the historical background to the psalm. In this case, the psalm's author, David, states that the historical setting, which prompted him to write this particular psalm, was his adulterous sin with Bathsheba.

2. My daughter was diagnosed in January 2004 with a form of leukemia called AML. Praise God, today she is perfectly healthy and leads a completely normal, active life. She is a walking miracle, but that story goes beyond the scope of this book.

3. The Churchill Centre, "We Shall Fight on the Beaches." http:// www.winstonchurchill.org.:4a/pages/index.cfm?pageid=393.

ACKNOWLEDGMENTS

ALL the contributing authors would like to express our gratitude and indebtedness to our wives (Crystal Charles, Marlean Felix, Joanna Hargrove, Hilda J. Kennedy, Sherry Kidd, Naomi Scott, Athena Sholar). For each of us, the familiar cliché that wives are the better half is both fitting and very true. Without their prayers and encouragement a project like this could never have been accomplished. In addition to our wives, there is a long list of others we need to thank for their input and help with this project.

We want to thank The Master's Seminary and the Los Angeles Bible Training School for their generous support for the Los Angeles Men's Bible Conference from which the idea for this book came about. The chapters of this book were preached as sessions in our annual 2005 conference entitled "Living Pure in an Impure World." To listen to those sermons, to contact the contributors, or to get more information about how to overcome secret sex wars, see www.secretsexwars.com.

We want to thank Lift Every Voice for their enthusiastic support for this writing project. We particularly appreciate their desire to promote this book and to help us get it into the hands of men in our communities.

We want to thank all of our family, friends, church members, and staff who read through drafts of our book giving us their helpful comments and corrections (Dennis Gundersen, Derek Clark, Renay Thompson, Alex Granados, Tim Carns, Alyce Campbell, Garry Knussman, David Stuart, Naomi Aidoo, Robert W. Fletcher, David Paul Morgan, Hilda J. Kennedy, George Hurtt, Scharmaine White, and TaVon Morrison).

We want to especially thank Naomi Scott for her tireless effort to serve as the proofreader of the initial drafts of each chapter, and Tom Rios for his insightful editorial comments.

We also want to thank you, the reader, for investing in this ministry tool. We pray that God will bless you through it and that you will be able to use it to encourage others to pursue grace-produced holiness.

Most of all we want to thank our Lord and Savior Jesus Christ for His soul-satisfying grace that wipes away all of our sins and gives us the power to overcome them.

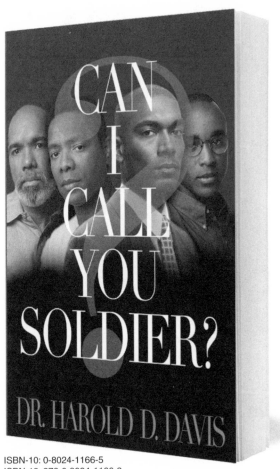

ISBN-10: 0-8024-1166-5
ISBN-13: 978-0-8024-1166-2

The war is at home and the battlefield is in the lives of our young men. In any community, and particularly in the black community, millions of young men feel the void of a role model. For every absent father, complacent leader, and passive bystander, there is a man who will step in and be a father figure—whether he is a trustworthy man of God or a dangerous enemy, someone will fill the void. It's up to us to win this battle and prepare the next generation to join in the fight. For the many men wondering how to win . . . *Can I Call You Soldier?* will be their strategy for victory.

by Dr. Harold Davis

Find it now at your favorite local or online bookstore.

www.LiftEveryVoiceBooks.com

ISBN-10: 0-8024-8989-3
ISBN-13: 978-0-8024-8989-0

In the eerie, classic television show *The Twilight Zone*, characters caught in the zone wanted nothing more than to return to normal life. Similarly, survivors of severe trauma fall into *The Trauma Zone*—a place they want to escape from, but can't. Some cannot move forward, feeling stuck and victimized by their past. Some cannot see the present, living in denial of what has happened. And others cannot learn from the past, repeating the same mistakes over and over. All of them find they can't cope with the overwhelming emotions that accompany trauma. Collins, a licensed psychologist with over 25 years experience in the healthcare field, believes there is a way out of the trauma zone and back to emotional health, a path he outlines in this practical, encouraging book.

by R. Dandridge Collins

Find it now at your favorite local or online bookstore.

www.LiftEveryVoiceBooks.com

ISBN-10: 0-8024-8801-3
ISBN-13: 978-0-8024-8801-5

This book traces the history of Christianity among African Americans and the development of the "Black Church"—those denominations created by, created for, and stewarded by African Americans. He examines the role the church has played politically and psychologically as well as spiritually in the lives of African Americans. This comprehensive psychological and spiritual look at an historic institution will be a valuable tool for both pastors and seminary professors.

by Lee June, Ph.D.
Find it now at your favorite local or online bookstore.

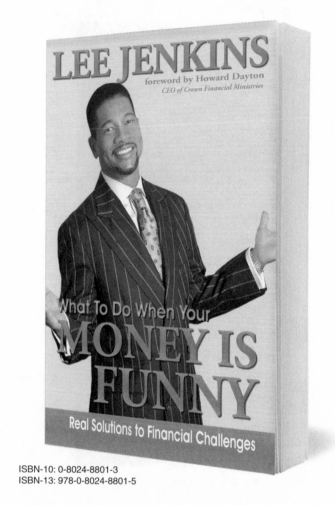

ISBN-10: 0-8024-8801-3
ISBN-13: 978-0-8024-8801-5

Strengthen your future. Empower your family. Improve your finances. These are the ministry goals of Lee Jenkins, Registered Investment Advisor, financial speaker, and author of Taking Care of Business. In his new book, Jenkins answers the most common questions he is asked at his financial conferences. He combines biblical wisdom, financial deftness, empathy, and encouragement to create a powerful guide for people looking to improve their financial circumstances God's way.

by Lee Jenkins
Find it now at your favorite local or online bookstore.

www.LiftEveryVoiceBooks.com

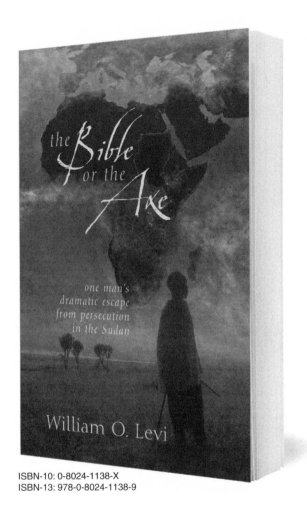

ISBN-10: 0-8024-1138-X
ISBN-13: 978-0-8024-1138-9

Exile. Persecution. Torture. The riveting story of one man's escape from the Sudan. By the muddy banks of the Kulo-jobi River, a young Sudanese boy is faced with a decision that will shape the rest of his life.

William Levi was born in southern Sudan as part of a Messianic Hebrew tribal group and spent the majority of his growing up years as a refugee running from Islamic persecution. He was eventually taken captive for refusing to convert to Islam and suffered greatly at the hands of his captor

by William O. Levi
Find it now at your favorite local or online bookstore.

www.LiftEveryVoiceBooks.com

The Negro National Anthem

Lift every voice and sing
Till earth and heaven ring,
Ring with the harmonies of Liberty;
Let our rejoicing rise
High as the listening skies,
Let it resound loud as the rolling sea.
Sing a song full of the faith that the dark past has taught us,
Sing a song full of the hope that the present has brought us,
Facing the rising sun of our new day begun
Let us march on till victory is won.

So begins the Black National Anthem by James Weldon Johnson in 1900. Lift Every Voice is the name of the joint imprint of The Institute for Black Family Development and Moody Publishers.

Our vision is to advance the cause of Christ through publishing African-American Christians who educate, edify, and disciple Christians in the church community through quality books written for African Americans.

Since 1988, the Institute for Black Family Development, a 501(c)(3) nonprofit Christian organization, has been providing training and technical assistance for churches and Christian organizations. The Institute for Black Family Development's goal is to become a premier trainer in leadership development, management, and strategic planning for pastors, ministers, volunteers, executives, and key staff members of churches and Christian organizations. To learn more about The Institute for Black Family Development write us at:

The Institute for Black Family Development
15151 Faust
Detroit, Michigan 48223

We hope you enjoy this book from Moody Publishers. Our goal is to provide high-quality, thought-provoking books and products that connect truth to your real needs and challenges. For more information on other books and products written and produced from a biblical perspective, go to www.moodypublishers.com or write to:

Moody Publishers/LEV
820 N. LaSalle Boulevard
Chicago, IL 60610
www.moodypublishers.com